# Food Writing ON THE RISE

Lyndsey Lefebvre

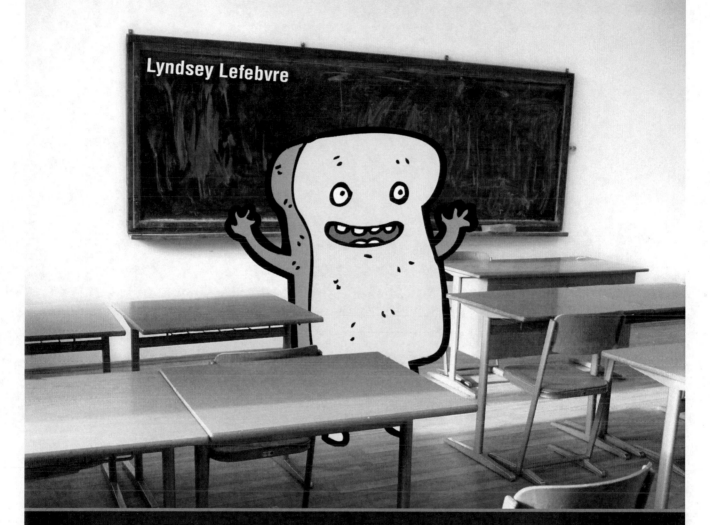

*Turning student loaves into* *gourmet rolls*

## Kendall Hunt
publishing company

**Kendall Hunt**
publishing company

www.kendallhunt.com
*Send all inquiries to:*
4050 Westmark Drive
Dubuque, IA 52004-1840

ISBN 978-1-4652-3157-4

Printed in the United States of America
10 9 8 7 6 5 4

# CONTENTS

# ACKNOWLEDGEMENTS

It is the goal of my book to bridge a gap in the classroom and the stomach of the student. I am so excited to see my dream become real, and I hope this book inspires educators to try reaching students in a way everyone can understand. This book has been the incarnation of the true monkey on my back, because I know that this focus, food, is in its prime time. I am so encouraged by the surge in other food-related texts that are becoming more mainstream and useful in the classroom. I am so thankful to my Acquisitions Editor, Jason McFaul, for his support and guidance. For Ryan Shrodt for his help on this project, and especially Kendall-Hunt Publishing for helping me get this type of learning experience in the hands of others.

Thank you to my local colleges that have shaped me as a student, Fullerton College and California State University, Fullerton. And thank you to the schools that have shaped my path as a teacher, Cerritos College, Orange County School of the Arts, Fullerton College, and Irvine Valley College. All of these wonderful learning institutions have allowed me to present this type of learning experiences for students; without those opportunities, this textbook would not be possible. A special thank you to all of my students who have been my proverbial guinea pigs for many of the assignments and learning experiences.

Thank you to all of the wonderful academics, teachers, educators, and foodies that have been writing about this important topic. I hope that students keep discovering more about their food worlds because of the work you do!

Thank you to my good friend and colleague, Michelle Stonis, for your wonderful wit and wisdom, and thank you for sharing your great mind with the students who will read this book! Thank you to Dr. Irena Praitis, for inspiring me to write for myself and for my dreams, and now look what I got myself into. It's absolutely awesome! Thank you for being part of it.

A special thank you to Heather MacDonald for being my second pair of eyes and ears. Keep throwing stuff real hard. To Susan Asch, the other half of my Lucy syndrome, thank you for always keeping me on my toes and my eyes on the prize. Thank you to Elena Harrington, for sharing oranges and mint in the Teaching Associate program at CSU Fullerton, I'm glad so many students will write better because of your great teaching moment!

This book would not be possible if it weren't for my husband, Robert, who has graciously let me slave away on my dream, which is to write a "first" book. Please continue your kindness for the subsequent books I hope to write in the future! Owen, you have always made everything in my life brighter, my Mini-Me. Sophie, thank you for naming Mr. Crusty. Thank you to my sister, Salina Marsh, for being by my side on the holidays and being willing to dice anything. To the Husband, Lefebvre, Marsh, and Chavez families for shaping my own food reality, thank you for being part of me.

# NOTE TO INSTRUCTORS

I was getting ready to become a teacher. Sitting in a coffee shop with my colleagues, discussing how we would take roll and design a syllabus, and around in circles we would spin discussing how to engage students through writing prompts. We had seen the standard questions that are often asked of students, such as "Describe a Significant Event," and "Take a position on a political issue." My own disdain about disingenuous writing topics made me realize that at least we could all agree that coffee was important to everyone. While discussing tipping waitresses, eating conventionally farmed eggs and margarine-laced toast, we talked about it over Thai food, and again when we would run into one another over yet another coffee on campus. It turns out that teachers and students having something in common—we both eat and are often caffeinated. Why couldn't students write about that?

Since we know we eat, and have survived long enough to make as far as we have, it dawned on me that bread was as worthy a topic as a political issue. Bread is political. It is socioeconomic. It is symbolic. Bread is a signifier. Bread is moldable at first and hardens over time; bread epitomizes the fabric of humanity. The human experience is a food experience. We all have experiences that reflect who we are from our dinner plate—and it is because of this connection to being human that I present this idea to you—you have something to say about food and so do your students.

The most prolific thing one of my professors in graduate school pointed out to me was that for as far as we knew, humans are the only animals that create stories. The first story in the Bible even has a food theme, Adam and Eve are in the Garden of Eden, and there is a fruity tree they aren't allowed to go near. From the dawn of man, it seems we are obsessed with what is forbidden for us to eat and what is deemed as okay to eat. While the assumption from this fallout is that Adam and Eve were forced into a life of working for their food, so have we been working for food stories that would help explain all of the human feelings that we encounter within life experience? When writing about individual food experiences, it becomes larger than the food in the story. The way that a person holds his or her food, chews it, accepts it, and rejects—it is all a story about who that person is or pretends to be. Prolific writers have been using food as a prop in narrative. The bread is passed, and that is a symbol; the fish was shared, and it becomes a pinnacle of the story; the drunkard loses control, and that itself tells a story. Writing about food is nothing new. Since the dawn of time recorded in narrative form, food has been a way of explaining human experience. Humans love to base everything on a story, and in this way, writing food stories is achievable.

It is great that we have people who are willing to help, which opens up the ability to write about another topic—helping others get food. In all studied culture, the passing of nourishment is how humans establish trust, beginning from birth. Being fed by others is an intimate venture that requires people to consider who is serving them is, what kinds of things they would present as edible to eat for their guest, and what about those we don't know? Are some people more generous with food than others? What is the state of helping people access healthy foods? Do communities care about the abilities of others to sustain a healthy diet? How communities feed each other not only says something about the community and state of affairs, the lack of this caring often signifies something else. The process of starving a community or poisoning a community has happened for the desire to control, and through the plate is a powerful way to reach people. As others eat wealthy rich meals, and others starve outside because they lack monetary means, there are those in between who are often the servants. They bring the food, sometimes in uniform, and they have decorum and processes for their steps, laying down the check, picking up the plate, and whom they will or will not serve. Those servants are often privy to a world they do not get to participate in. Sometimes they are not employees, and they are parents. And with all of these people serving us food, ensuring the supply, and allowing us choices in the market-place, that leaves the question of how long the food you eat will still be there.

The latest buzzword, as of the last decade, is "sustainability." Live long and prosper. Be around for a long time in the same form. For agribusiness, this buzzword has been a difficult acceptance of applying a standard to how people view the impact of what they eat. They bring it to the stores for us to buy, and they have been sustaining that for almost 60 years. Many accounts of today's food system recount that it is unsustainable. We can't keep up with growing populations, loss of farmland, and changes to urban areas. But if you were never required to search for food in the "hunter-gatherer" sense, why would you care in the first place? How do you guarantee that your next meal will be there for you? How to you sustain your own food supply? These are questions our students might not even consider without this chance.

This book is meant as a supplement for a college-level writing course. I have been using themed food writing courses for classes that are for second language learning students, students who need help with grammar and paragraphs, basic essay writing, and advanced rhetoric. This book is intended to touch on several course objectives, while supplementing a larger course curriculum. Each chapter can be tilted to other types of writing assignments or topical focuses based on the students and the instructor.

Part of the strategy with this type of theme for a class is that students are learning to write by learning about themselves and something immediate around them. College is often full of things that feel far reaching for students, and when they get the opportunity to be an expert in something, they take up the calling, the challenge, and you will be surprised about how they can surprise you. Some of the excerpts in the book revolve around my particular locale of Orange County, California; however, I would encourage an instructor adopting this textbook to ensure he or she includes personal experiences in the course discussion.

If you are teaching a food-writing course, and are interested in contributing to a future edition, I would love to talk to you about your food-writing strategies in the classroom. I hope one day students have the opportunity to use food as a medium for education from kindergarten to college and thank you for using this book for the powers of eating and helping that goal reach students.

# INTRODUCTION

The purpose of this book is to assist you through a basic composition course using food-themed assignments. They range from long to short, simple to complex, and they offer students the opportunity to form their own opinions and ideas based on the evidence of their diet and choices. This book will ask students to consider their world at a local level and within a global context. Students will develop analytical and critical thinking skills that transcend the composition course and transfer to home, body, school, society, and culture.

You might be thinking, "How can I really write all about food? It is just three meals a day." Then you might consider something as simple as the first meal of the day, breakfast. What do you eat for breakfast? Do you skip breakfast despite the old adage of breakfast being "the most important meal of the day"? Do you get excited when you hear of a new scientific study that promises a strong start to the day based on what you ate in the morning? So when you realize that you are going to eat this meal, breakfast, what exactly do you eat? Do you eat fortified breakfast cereal with cartoon characters on the box? Does it remind you of your childhood Saturday mornings? Who bought you the cereal in the first place? Did you ever get into fights about what kind of cereal was good to eat, and which was not? What if the idea of American breakfast cereal is foreign to you because you eat traditional ethnic food for breakfast? Maybe you eat more "breakfast-y" foods like waffles and pancakes; do you know where they originated? What about the bacon and sausage on the side, how did you ever think eating pork was okay, but you might turn up your nose at spicy crickets in a blue corn tortilla? Let's look closer into your bacon and think about where the animal was born, raised, and processed into your food on your plate, does knowing this information change your view of what you are eating? What does it mean to eat "Facon" instead of Bacon? Are there side effects to a plant-based soy diet? What are you going to wash it all down with? Milk? Homogenized? Pasteurized? Grass-fed Pastured? Corn-fed Feedlot? Hand milked? Hooked to a machine? Why can't you just know these things by looking at the labels of the food you purchase? Why don't you know more about your breakfast?

In addition to stories about food, it is another issue in our modern age that defining food is becoming an ever-increasing labor of love. The once simplistic story of denim overalls on a farmer with a pitchfork bringing eggs to the local supermarket is not the reality of how we define our food processes. And how do we define eggs anyway? How are the lines drawn for acceptable definitions of food and the unacceptable foods? Who writes the definitions? When you include the issue of comparing and contrasting food products, or how the same food experience can be perceived as different to someone else, it becomes an endless opportunity for paralleling food issues and stories.

People have been "cooking" for thousands of years, and those particular "cookers" who have achieved high levels of success deserve scrutiny and admiration. Who decides what kind of food is tasty? How do you know if you have talent in the kitchen? What is the role of high-level cooking personalities and their influence on the diets of the people who listen to them? What kinds of ingredients do they recommend to their audiences? Are you able to cook for yourself, or do you depend on someone to help you out with that on a daily basis?

My hope, as a writing teacher, is that when you leave your College-Level Writing Course, you feel like you have more to say about the world than when you started. If you have never thought about your diet, or if you obsess, this book will help guide you through writing—via your stomach. It begins in your mouth to taste it, but to write it, it begins in your brain. Maybe for you, it begins with braving brains on your plate, or to confront the brains you conflict with, or the way your brain is hard-boiled.

Where is the bread? The international symbol of sharing—my title indicates that when you are finished with this book, you might consider yourself more *gourmand* than loaf-y. You might think you are more sophisticated about the table and more informed than those around you. But, you should always remember:

Our varied relationship to the food we eat is as sure as death and taxes.

Your reality will never be the next generations' food reality. I hope over your courses you slow down and think about what kind of bread you are making for this world and what kinds of slices come off your loaf.

This book is an attempt to help you to write by thinking critically about what is already in front of you. With all of the other disciplines that you might take in your future college career, this type of book will end up touching on everything else. Food is science, humanities, machines, ethics, philosophy, business, art, sport, and administration. You are here because you've been eating so far, and after this book, I hope you feel confident to write about your own relationships to the world that you've been swallowing.

# PART 1

# KNEADING WHAT YOU KNOW ABOUT WRITING

# Writing Food Stories (Getting Started Writing About Food)

"Tell Me What You Eat and I Tell You Who You Are."

— (Brillat-Savarin)

In order to get started writing about food, the first step is to realize that you're not really writing about food. What is food anyway? A bunch of molecules? Nutrients? Sustenance? In your daily experience, does food grow on a tree or out of the ground, or is it something more abstract because you've never thought about it before? Our individuation and evolution as living beings shows itself through the multitude of ways in which food is represented in our daily lives—fancy food, express food, fast food, junk food.

What is food, and what does it really mean to us? This question, when grappled with by scholars, reveals an un-stunning answer when we consider how each person's individual food history is different from another. You cannot have the same history with food as someone else. Did you grow up with an *Abuela* that taught you to make *albondigas*? Did you spend every Sunday at the same coffee shop with your grandfather? Did you choke on a chicken bone when you were a baby? Every experience you have had is unique to someone else's. Because of this, what you find most important about food may not be what others feel is essential. Maybe you need to have a specific type of drink when you go out with your friends. This preference can be read as a symbol of a bigger point of who you are. When your aunt comments on the amount of food on your plate for holiday dinners, she is not just talking about the physical mounds on your plate. She is talking about what your servings signify—maybe you are concerned about gaining weight, or you do not care and are gorging on the good stuff. Every day, hopefully, three times a day, your dietetic culture is perpetuated through food choices that you do or do not make. If you do not eat three times a day, which is the Western norm for eating, that can become something to write about as well. The food you choose to eat on a daily basis and on special occasions says something about you. Your rejection of food says something too. But what does it say?

# HAVE YOU EVER:

Sent food back at a restaurant? Asked your parental figure to prepare a special meal for you? Been revived by someone's home cooking when you are sick? Eaten something after not having it for a while? Had to attend an awkward holiday dinner?

The way we eat and view our food and eating customs reveals a lot about the characters we portray in writing.

## Drawing Exercise:

Draw a picture of a person being a picky eater:

Draw a picture of a baby and a first plate of spaghetti:

Draw school children having lunch:

Draw a fancy dinner:

**Respond:** What are the visual cues that tell a story? How do specific details make the story come alive through your picture?

Compare your drawings with a classmate and compare and contrast your pictures with the following:

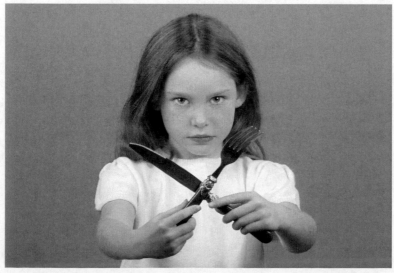

Image © Cheryl Casey, 2011. Used under license from Shutterstock, Inc.

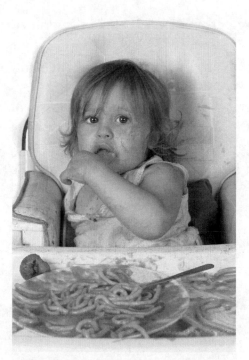

Image © GraÃ§a Victoria, 2011. Used under license from Shutterstock, Inc.

Image © Lisa F. Young, 2011. Used under license from Shutterstock, Inc.

Image © Martin Maun, 2011. Used under license from Shutterstock, Inc.

Does your picture reflect anything personal? What kind of equipment is present in the picture? What kind of tone does the scene show?

Does the school lunch picture match any of your notions about eating at school? Do you have similar ideas about this scene as your own drawing?

Does the fancy dinner picture provide you enough details to know the restaurant rating? What about the menu for the evening? Does the fancy dinner include any details about who would eat there?

Sometimes, the larger narrative of what it means to participate in food experiences is reflected in similar ways, no matter what type of individual experiences you may be used to; those experiences that become universal, often carrying details that transcend and connect largely with people who have similar experiences.

Everyone's attitudes and relationship with eating is different. And, it is this difference that makes it interesting. If every day the standard breakfast, lunch, and dinner could be understood as a beginning, middle, and end, then the likeness between meals starts to sound like a story.

## WHAT MAKES A FOOD STORY?

Paul Cobley, who wrote an extensive critical lens on Narrative, breaks down the structure of our stories:

"'[S]tory consists of all the events which are to be depicted. 'Plot' is the chain of causation which dictates that these events are somehow linked and that they are therefore to be depicted in relation to each other. 'Narrative' is the showing or the telling of these events and the mode selected for that to take place" (*Narrative*, 5–6).

So, this means that the Story is how the events are told. Plot is the step-by-step progression of the events. And finally, Narrative is how you show or tell the events.

Consider the children's classic, *Hansel and Gretel* (which can be found online in text format).

Image © lineartestpilot, 2011. Used under license from Shutterstock, Inc.

If you were going to break this story down based on Cobley's model of Narrative:

**What is the Story?**

**What is the Plot?**

**What is the Narrative?**

**Discuss your answers with the class!**

When writing food stories, it becomes important to consider how your reader will understand your deliberate plot points, the narrative information that gives the story shape and unique detail, and a story that has purpose.  There are old sayings about writing: "You can't write about what you don't know." "You should write from your own perspective." "You can only talk about subjects you know a lot about." While some of the logic behind these statements refers to students being aware that they need to have interest in what they are writing about, it is also fair to say that there will be times where you might have to write about something you don't care too much about. When you need to write in narrative form, realizing that all stories have these intricate parts that make them have form, you can see how it makes their details significant, and the flow of their story successful and purposeful.

Cobley, Paul. Narrative (The New Critical Idiom). New York: Routledge, 2003. Book.

# WRITING YOUR OWN FOOD STORY

Students sometimes fear that they do not have enough life content for their food stories. However, the great act of about writing a food story is the opportunity to create significance in something that everyone does on a daily basis, and if they do not eat, that is significant as well.

**Take the following food inventory for yourself:**

- When was the last time your parent(s) fed you, either by cooking or purchasing your food?
- When was the last time you prepared your own food and what did you prepare for yourself?
- Has anyone taught you something about the food you eat, or food that you would make?
- Do you have early stories about eating? Are there pictures of any of the incidents?
- Did you have a childhood food that you refused to eat?
- Did you have a favorite food that you liked so much you mispronounced it?
- Did you refuse food as a child and get punished for it?
- Has an adult ever made you to eat something?

- Have you ever been forced to eat food that you didn't want to eat?
- Do particular people in your life pressure you to eat certain foods?
- Do you have a food phobia?
- Do you eat everything in sight and love to be adventurous? Is this annoying to other people?
- Have you ever had a confrontation while eating a meal with someone?
- Has anyone invited you to coffee, that wasn't really for "coffee"?
- Have you ever tried to feed someone food that you made? Did they accept it or reject it?
- Have you ever introduced your cultural or ethnic food to someone who was unfamiliar with it?

What makes these stories significant? What kinds of details would need to be present to engage the average reader? Compare your answers with your class. How many of them have these kinds of experiences?

# THIS DAY'S FOOD

Nathaniel Hawthorne

Wednesday, August 24th, 1842.

I left my Sophie's arms at five o'clock this morning, to catch some fish for dinner. On my way through the orchard, I shook our summer apple-tree, and ate the golden apple which fell from it. Methinks these early apples, which come as a golden promise before the treasures of autumnal fruit, are almost more delicious than anything that comes afterwards. We have but one such tree in our orchard; but it supplies us with a daily abundance, and promises to do so for at least a week to come. Meantime, other trees begin to cast their ripening windfalls upon the grass; and when I taste them, and perceive their mellowed flavor and blackening seeds. I feel somewhat overwhelmed with the impending bounties of Providence. I suppose Adam, in Paradise, did not like to see his fruits decaying on the ground, after he had watched them through the sunny days of the world's first summer. However, insects, at the worst, will hold a festival upon them; so that they will not be thrown away, in the great scheme of nature. Moreover, I have one advantage over the primeval Adam, inasmuch as there is a chance of disposing of my superfluous fruits among people who inhabit no Paradise of their own.

Passing a little way down along the river-side. I threw in my line, and soon drew out one of the smallest possible fish. It seemed to be a pretty good morning for the angler—an autumnal coolness in the air; a clear sky, but with a fog along the lowlands and on the surface of the river, which a gentle breeze sometimes condensed into wreaths. At first, I could barely discern the opposite shore of the river; but as the sun arose, the vapors gradually dispersed, till only a warm smoky tint was left along the water's surface. The farm-houses, across the river, made their appearance out of the dusky cloud:—the voices of boys were heard, shouting to the cattle as they drove them to pasture;—a mower whet his scythe, and set to work in a neighboring meadow. Meantime, I continued to stand on the oozy margin of the stream, beguiling the little fish; and though the scaly inhabitants of our river partake somewhat of the character of their native element, and are but sluggish biters, still I contrived to pull out not far from two dozen. They were all bream—a broad, flat, almost circular fish, shaped a good deal like a flounder, but swimming on their edges, instead of their flat sides. As far as mere pleasure is concerned, it is hardly worth while to fish in our river, it is so much like angling in a mud-puddle; and one does not attach the idea of freshness and purity to the fish, as we do to those which inhabit swift, transparent streams, or haunt the shores of the great briny deep. Standing on the weedy margin, and throwing the line over the elder-bushes that dip into the water, it seems as if we could catch nothing but frogs and mud-turtles, or reptiles akin to them; and even when a fish of reputable aspect is drawn out, you feel a shyness about

touching him. As to our river, my little wife expressed its character admirably, last night; she said "it was too lazy to keep itself clean." I might write pages and pages, and only obscure the impression which this brief sentence conveys. Nevertheless, we made bold to eat some of my fish for breakfast, and found them very savory; and the rest shall meet with due entertainment at dinner, together with some shell-beans, green corn, and cucumbers from our garden; so that this day's food comes directly and entirely from beneficent Nature, without the intervention of any third person between her and us.

*The American Notebooks* (1972; written 1842)

## Discussion Questions:

1. How is the food that Hawthorne finds for himself different than the way you find your food?

2. What is the impact of Hawthorne's religious views? How does that affect the way he thinks about food and eating?

# FOOD AND SENSORY DETAILS

**Try this:**

Gather up the following food items:

Orange Slices

Mint Leaves

Coffee Beans

Image © Valentyn Volkov, 2011. Used under license from Shutterstock, Inc.

Image © dionisvera, 2011. Used under license from Shutterstock, Inc.

Image © GMEVIPHOTO, 2011. Used under license from Shutterstock, Inc.

Now, consider each food item separately and write about each of them. Prepare yourself to write at least a paragraph.

When you write about Oranges, you are forbidden from using the word "Orange." With Mint, you cannot use "Mint," and with Coffee, you can't say "Coffee." And you can't add a –y at the end either, because that is not inventive, and practically cheating. Devote yourself to a paragraph each and write against the following question:

If you were going to describe an orange, mint, or coffee to a person who had never tasted, smelled, or seen these items, what language would you use to describe what they are? Write a letter to someone in a distant land to explain what these items are and what use they have.

# DON'T DRINK THE KOOL-AID

Michelle Stonis

It's inexpensive. It's reportedly loved by kids. It's Kool-Aid, the beverage that simply needs water and a good stir in order to induce smiles on kids' and parents' faces alike. Or so the marketing goes. Knowing the etymology and history of the Kool-Aid cliché, "Don't drink the Kool-Aid," is more than good trivia game fodder. Studying Kool-Aid and its related stories are prime examples of how food can be written about.

The platitude, "Don't drink the Kool-Aid," has nothing to do with disliking the sweetened beverage and the large smiley-faced pitcher that has been its logo since 1954. This cliché stems from two historical events. In 1968, author Tom Wolfe wrote *The Electric Kool-Aid Acid Test*, a nonfiction novel in which he chronicled the psychoactive drug experimentation of hippies, led by Ken Kesey and the Merry Pranksters. After some partygoers had a bad reaction to the LSD-laced beverage, Wolfe begged his mentally unstable friend to not drink the Kool-Aid, a statement that was reinvented into a cliché that advocated against mindlessly going along with the crowd. This saying and its real-life association with Kool-Aid was further reinforced when deadly cyanide-laced Kool-Aid was given in 1978 to 909 members of the Peoples Temple, a church led by Reverend Jim Jones as they sought to create a utopian socialist society known as Jonestown in Guyana, South America. The Jonestown Kool-Aid was forcefully given to many people during the mass suicide-murder, which included infants being given the bitter-tasting Kool-Aid by syringe.

Primary sources, meaning historical material that was created during the time period, are useful for learning about the history of a particular food item as well as analyzing the ways in which food has been written about, and given symbolic meaning, over time. Secondary sources, meaning material interpreting and discussing primary sources are helpful for learning from experts and gaining a broad understanding of the topic at hand. The primary or secondary status of a source depends on the topic of inquiry. In the case of writing about Kool-Aid, Wolfe's book and the Jonesboro tapes are primary sources while a museum article about the beverage is a secondary source. My own tasting of Kool-Aid or memories of having a summer Kool-Aid stand could also be relevant primary sources.

In 1927, Edward Perkins of Hastings, Nebraska, changed his liquid Fruit Smack recipe from 1920 into sweet beverage powder mix packets that sold for ten cents apiece through the mail. However, Perkins most likely never imagined that Kool-Ade (later renamed Kool-Aid) would eventually be known by a cliché stating *not* to consume his beverage. In an effort to avoid drinking the metaphorical Kool-Aid, we should continue to become more aware of the significance of these common nutritional items and the meanings of the stories that contain them.

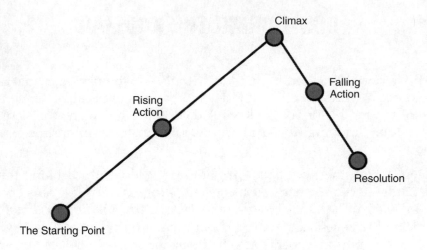

# BRAINSTORMING FOR FOOD NARRATIVES

Writing a narrative follows a basic structure: The Starting Point, Rising Action, Climax, and Resolution. Sometimes the shape of the peak varies, but generally there is still the same points, stories have a place to start, have action to follow, a major point that helps resolve and end the story.

Think about your favorite Disney movie (if you have one), and see how this arc is applied to that story.

Now write out the main plot points:

**The Starting Point:**

**Climax:**

**Resolution:**

Think back to one of the earlier pictures featuring a baby eating spaghetti or the group of kids eating lunch—can you think of a story arc that would correlate with the picture? Using one of the pictures as an example, write out a story arc.

Looking at the arc below, you can add to your story arc the upswing of the arc, called the rising action, and then the point on the downward slop, referred to as the reversal. The rising action is the point in the story where there is a connection from the start to the poignant point of the narrative. The reversal is the point when the narrative starts to shift and change to end up in the resolution.

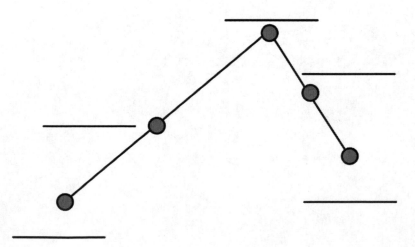

# BAGUETTE OR ROLL?

Sometimes when students are given a writing assignment, one of the most daunting aspects can be the length requirement. Soon enough the comfortable days of five-paragraph essays will be long gone. But, sometimes students don't realize that there is power in telling stories succinctly. Short stories and flash fiction (100–250 words) are all the rage in some creative writing circuits.

**Now, create a short narrative about the following pictures:**

Image © Glenda M. Powers, 2011. Used under license from Shutterstock, Inc.

Image © Jaimie Duplass, 2011. Used under license from Shutterstock, Inc.

Image © Blend Images, 2011. Used under license from Shutterstock, Inc.

## ASSIGNMENT 1:

One of the most common food stories stems from the idea of accepting a food that you might not normally eat, or rejecting a food because you don't want to eat it and then suffering the consequences. For this essay, focus on a time that you ate a food that you would have accepted, or a time that you rejected food and refused to eat it. Be sure that you adhere to the classic storytelling arc and give significant details about your experience, your setting, the food, and the personal interactions that will make your story interesting and successful.

## ASSIGNMENT 2:

Instead of standard essay writing, for this assignment, you will write courses. Think of your essay as being three different courses for your reader. Using methods of storytelling, use each course to present a memory that is significant to you. In the memory, an aspect of food should be included, using concrete and supporting details. Each separate piece of writing should NOT have an Introduction or Conclusion, but instead, should be written in paragraph form with an immediate start to the narrative. Each "course" should be about a page, or slightly longer, but should not be longer than 1 ½ to 2 pages each. Each memory, or story, should be succinct and short, emphasizing important details and significance. Why is the food you are writing about important and worth showing your reader? Does the memory have a lesson? Are larger societal issues underlying your memory? Does the past have a connection to the future? You decide the significance and serve it up. This essay will require you to think outside the box, there are no introductions, conclusions, or thesis, just deep content.

# VOCABULARY TIP

Do you know basic food vocabulary? You might be surprised about the diverse language that makes up food vocabulary. In this book you will find helpful words that will be defined for you, but sometimes you may root around to find your own answers. If someone *beat* an egg, would you know what that meant? What about *baste*? Do you know what *fennel* is? Learning more about the words associated with food is a helpful way to build your vocabulary—which ends up being helpful in other disciplines as well! If you have the desire to know what maltodextrin is, you have the gumption to investigate any topic! At the end of each chapter you will find a few words with definitions that you might not be familiar with. There will also be spaces for you to input your own vocabulary for each chapter. A wise teacher once told me that you cannot learn vocabulary by putting a book to your forehead. Learning vocabulary is an active act–and starting with what you eat will lead you into know more about other subjects as well.

# VOCABULARY

Plot: Chain of events happening in a string. (Beginning Middle End)

Story: The method of delivering the details of the events.

Narrative: The showing of the story.

Cliché: A stereotyped expression

# Defining Food

Meet Nancy. Nancy has a problem. She won't eat anything without feeling comfortable that she knows exactly what she is eating. She demands that her food be familiar to her, nothing unrecognizable, nothing fancy, just food. Do you know what Nancy eats? If she were to ask you to make something for her, would you know what not to put in it? There are times when there are people who will not eat food unless they feel like they have thoroughly evaluated and understood what it is they are eating. But where does Nancy draw the line for understanding and knowing what to eat and not to eat? How can she decide what is food, and what is not food? She might refuse mushrooms because they are fungi or dislike cilantro because of the smell. These are things that Nancy does not consider edible or food. But what about you? How do you define the *edible* and *inedible*? What is food to you?

## DEFINITION TIME!

**What is your definition of food?**

In recent years, much public attention and debate has poured into what is considered food. Some ideas about food are broad, and many people come to agree and accept that the definitions are the widely accepted truth. Good bananas are yellow. But, it is possible that some bananas, which are not standard bananas, are better when green. We can mostly agree what bananas are, what they look like, and what the ideal color for them is, but there are some bananas that escape this definition, like plantains or burro bananas. This doesn't just happen with food—it happens with all subjects. When students are asked to define things like *truth, justice,* and *love,* the question assumes a relationship shared between students with those topics. It takes time, effort, and academic fortitude not to repeat the long-established clichés about how love is patient, kind and other vague concepts. The challenge with writing to define food is making sure you provide your reader the supporting details necessary to connect with your subject, showing how flour, yeast, and some water can turn into some kind of bread. If you define your diet as incomplete without eating crickets, then your definition is your own experience and detailed support material. Despite your steady diet of crickets, you might still understand the broader experience of people who have aversions to eating bugs for lunch. The writer must always consider both sides—the writer who is seeking the reader to comprehend and the reader who is only able to understand based on what the writer writes.

For example:

In this square below, draw a picture of a farm scene. (What kind of farm you might ask? Close your eyes. Imagine a giant chalkboard and the word **FARM**. Now draw that farm that came to your head. Don't question it, just draw it.)

**Consider the following:**

What color is the barn?

Are there chickens? What color are they?

Is there a person in your scene?

Compare your answers with your classmates. You might find that although everyone knows what a farm is, it is the minute details that can create a difference in how you visualize your farm.

Are there any similarities in the answers?

How many people included a white chicken?

How many people have a red barn?

Is the person in the picture wearing denim?

## Discussion Questions:

What makes a farm a farm?

What are the inspirations for your idea of a farm?

Does specific evidence in your farm show that you have common ideas with your classmates?

Do you have specific details that are unique to your farm? Why did these unique images appear?

# WHAT IS LOCAL FOOD?

Find five food items in your kitchen. On this map, place dots that indicate their source and a star to indicate your location.

Draw your neighborhood within a half a mile. Indicate every food source within that range by dots. Draw your self as a star in your neighborhood. (Hint: GoogleMaps)

Respond:

1. How far did your farthest food product come from?

2. Of the items in your home, which one do you eat most often, and where does it come from?

3. Can any of your five items be found more locally than others?

4. What kinds of options are local to you?

5. Is there a place within this radius that you eat at regularly?

6. Are they corporate chains or Mom and Pop businesses?

7. Have you eaten at any of these places? How many?

8. How many of these places would you never go to, and why?

Once you consider this exercise . . .

Define: Local Food on one side of the column. What does it mean to you to eat locally? How far is too far? How would eating locally limit your diet?

After you give your definition, look at the Wikipedia entry for "Local Food."

1. How does your definition and Wikipedia's definition compare and contrast?

# DICING UP WORDS

In today's often politically correct world that commands the most precise definitions, it is ironic that our supermarkets are full of contradictions, word traps, and misaligned information.

Without looking up any of these words, write your own definitions for the terms below, based on how they sound or what they would indicate to you.

Animal:

Battery Cage:

Bycatch:

CAFO:

Comfort Food:

Are these words that you can find in a grocery store? Do people at the grocery store know their definitions? Can you find any information about these words on food packaging?

When you consider how the aforementioned words by themselves seem foreign yet unobtrusive, how they are then explained through the author's definition can change your original idea of how to define these words. You might believe that an apple is one thing,

Your ideas and connotations about these words might have one slant, but to someone else they might have another. Jonathan Safran Foer spent several years investigating the reasons behind eating animals, so much so that his vocabulary was expanded and reshaped. When you investigate these words, how does your own definition become more acute or accurate?

Foer, Jonathan Safran. Eating Animals. New York: Hatchette Book Group, 2009. Book.

So, let's think about an even more complicated question:

# WHAT IS FOOD?

When Michael Pollan gives his wise foodie advice for good eating as "Eat food. Not too much. Mostly plants" (*In Defense of Food*, 1), it would seem like food is easy to find, it is easy to eat the right amount, and that everyone knows how to identify edible plants. But, the reality is that many people consider different things to be food than others.

For example, look at the following pictures and decide if the image depicts a "food" or not a food.

Image © Valentyn Volkov, 2011. Used under license from Shutterstock, Inc.

Image © Margaret M Stewart, 2011. Used under license from Shutterstock, Inc.

Image © Burhan Bunardi Xie, 2011. Used under license from Shutterstock, Inc.

Image © chrisdouglas123, 2011. Used under license from Shutterstock, Inc.

Image © LittleMiss, 2011. Used under license from Shutterstock, Inc.

Image © Pavzyuk Svitlana, 2011. Used under license from Shutterstock, Inc.

In response to the images above, discuss with your classmates what you all agree is edible, and what you believe is not.

Pollan, Michael. In Defense of Food: An Eater's Manifesto. New York: Penguin Books, 2008.

# ACTIVITY

Have you ever been grocery shopping with someone you don't live with? Ever paid attention to the things that person buys versus what you consider regular staples in your house? Follow someone along for his or her trip, and write about how his or her definition of food is different from or similar to yours!

# CHANGING DEFINITIONS

Just like one would expect fine restaurants to use the "new" and seasonal, so is language. Some words have a season, like certain bibliographic standards, which change and morph over time. Sometimes certain ways of citing source information require placement in the essay a particular way. You might get used to that form, then the rule would change as fast as you change majors. Students who are successful in college understand that the modes and requirements that are presented to students have a way of changing or being hard to pin down exactly. It is important to remain current, every time you are asked to write, with the most current methods available.

It is also important to recognize how Food Studies now factors into Cultural Studies. Recently, the American Psychological Association amended the APA stylebook to include food-specific ways to cite information (Article can be found in course website!).

While the APA is updating its style, there is also cause to examine the definitions that are being currently established. One of the biggest demands of the modern college student is to leave the experience with more questions than answers. A professor from my school once said that if college was not a life-altering experience, then you might want to get a refund. College is supposed to engage you in what you think you believe and open your own ideas and possibilities for applying your personal changes to the world around you. Just like the MLA and APA, which change their styles and expect you to be current, the world is expecting you to change and be current, a true point of education—and it applies in the food world as well. When we are beginning to look at what we eat critically, we should consider what it means to change and how we use this information to stay current. We become active and engaged in the world around us, because we are going to keep eating. But, college ends up teaching you that you don't have to swallow everything that you are being served.

For example, Gustavo Arellano, a writer hailing from Anaheim, smack dab in the middle of Orange County, California, researches the origins of Mexican food from around America. From this undertaking, his own investigations into the given definitions by the Oxford English Dictionary, considered by many to be the gold standard of the English language, showed that those definitions need reworking. By having a platform to share this writing, he is engaging his audience in the ideas of questioning the powers that be that declare the origin of the word "taquito."

"Five (Largely Inaccurate) Oxford English Dictionary Entries for Mexican Foods." OCWeekly.com. Village Voice, Web. 14 Dec. 2011.

**Define for yourself:**

**Your cultural cuisine:**

 **Chicken:**

 **Breakfast:**

 **Dinner:**

 **Dessert:**

 **A "sweet":**

 **Fruit:**

 **Slaughterhouse:**

 **Inedible:**

## ASSIGNMENT 1

Consider a food definition that you feel really comfortable with. You feel like you know what "x" is, through and through. While considering this one item, investigate the definition of the word and show how your evidence supports or refutes your initial definitions. Has the item changed definition? When did the change occur? How has the item become relevant to you? And how has your definition changes or stayed the same?

## ASSIGNMENT 2

Find a word that is associated with food that you know nothing about. It could be a vegetable you've never eaten or a packaged ingredient that you do not know how to pronounce, let alone where it comes from. Write an essay that shows a historical definition of how this item came to be called what it is called, where it came from, and how many different associations come with the word itself.

## ASSIGNMENT 3

Have you ever written down all of the ways you participate with food for a set amount of time? Diet experts say, "you are what you eat," but if you record all of your interactions with food, eating, buying, cooking, sharing, for a week, what would people think about your relationship with the world? Do you eat out a lot? Do you only like a particular person's cooking? Do you fend for yourself? Record your habits for a week, then construct a food biography that explains who you are, based on your food choices. How do your food habits define you?

# VOCABULARY

**Define:** Not only a means of identification, but also a way a human specifies something.

**CAFO:** Concentrated Animal Feedlot Operation.

**Vegan:** A lifestyle that avoids animal products, including food, medicine, and clothing.

**Maple Syrup:** Sap from maple trees.

**Local Food:** A term that indicates a desire to eat food made within a personal circumference.

**Bycatch:** The unfortunate side effect of buying wild-caught fish. It's all the extras that are thrown over board as waste.

**Locavore:** Someone who purposely eats "local."

**Battery Cage:** A cage system for keeping small animals in small places.

**Comfort Food:** Food that is supposed to comfort.

_____

_____

_____

_____

**3**
Chapter

# Considering All Parts: Analysis and Food

Now that we have experienced defining, let's talk about defining one of the most popular foods in America:

## WHAT IS PIZZA? WRITE YOUR DEFINITION.

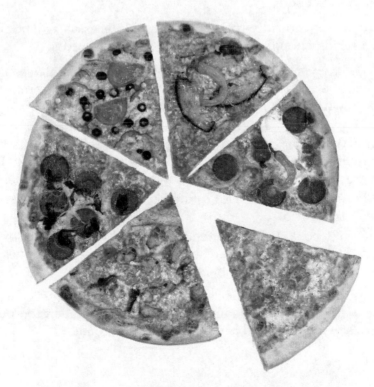

So, did your definition include:

**Crust? / Sauce? / Cheese?**

Did you specify toppings?

Everyone knows the basic idea of pizza, but what about those specific variations?

Thin crust? Hand tossed? Stuffed crust? Pan?

Marinara sauce? Alfredo sauce? Olive oil?

Mozzarella? Goat cheese? Feta cheese? Parmesan?

It just so happens that pizza has plenty to do with writing, because essays are just like pizzas.

We all know that essays have basic parts. We know they have sentences and paragraphs, and they need to include a thesis statement, but how these essay ingredients are presented creates a different essay pizza every time you write it, bake it. You know what I mean.

# CRUST

The foundation to your essay is your Thesis Statement. It is important that the rest of your essay be connected to this statement, just like all of the toppings and parts of a pizza loaded on top. In order for those ingredients to exist as "pizza," your crust should be solid and reassuring to everything you load up on top of it. Think of your crust having variables:

Sometimes a thin crust thesis doesn't give enough explanation or specific information.
Examples:

- Bread is a good thing to have at the table.
- Pizza is popular everywhere.
- I like food that tastes good.

While these statements could be indicative of what the rest of the essay will be about, they don't really say anything enticing or strong enough to be able to entertain the reader.

Sometimes an overstuffed crust is tasty, but as a thesis statement, it creates complication. If you can't tell where the toppings start and the crust ends, the overlap can leave a professor wondering by the end of your first few ideas what and when is the actual point of your essay.
Examples:

- Cruelty to animals is often reflected in the kitchen, and the slaughterhouses don't help matters much with their allowed exploitation and profit mongering. Keeping backyard chickens is a great way to eat eggs for free and watch the rooster chase your children.
- Bread is good to have at the table for dinner, is found in breakfast food, and is used by every culture in the world.
- When chefs learn to cook, they are often astounded by the amount of food safety regulations they must follow. Often they are taught proper knife techniques, but they do not understand front of the house manners.

After reading each of these, I slapped myself because I was sure each sentence was six different essays. A thesis statement is deliberate and all encompassing. If all of these ideas on their own provide your support, then your thesis statement would benefit from being broader.

There is that "just-right" crust, the hand tossed. You might start thin, but you might add too much dough. But if you knead it out, you can get a thesis that is clear and concise and to the point.

Examples:

- Bread has historical significance as a symbol of friendship over the eating table.
- When animals are raised for food in stressful environments, the meat tastes like rubber, has higher incidents of food-borne illness, and lacks flavor.
- Popular chefs often advertise their use of organic and local ingredients to attract customers who care about the environment.

Your thesis statement should contain two parts, the subject that you are writing about, and the reason or slant of your paper about it. A thesis statement that has been massaged enough to include only enough information to sum up the paper in one sentence are often the strongest and can make writing the rest of the essay far easier.

Image © Nayashkova Olga, 2011. Used under license from Shutterstock, Inc.

# PRACTICE

Construct one of each kind of thesis:

**Thin Crust:**

**Stuffed Crust:**

**Hand Tossed:**

Image © gosphotodesign, 2011. Used under license from Shutterstock, Inc.

If you lay down the right crust, then adding sauce can begin.

There is a difference in quality when discussing the perfect pizza, and the laying of sauce is the main connection to the rest of the pizza. In an essay, paragraphs are perform this same function. Just like the spooning of sauce from a ladle on the dough, paragraphs are spread over the essay, each one different and unique, yet cohesive to the crust below it.

Ideally, we want the sauce around the dough, evenly, and without notice. Paragraphs work the same way in an essay. Aesthetically looking at your essay by printing the whole thing out, laying it on your bread board, and noticing which paragraphs are longer, which are shorter, and which are just right, is as important as smoothing with the back of a ladle.

### Let's Characterize Sauce

Thin Sauce: Paragraphs are too short and do not have enough detail to stand on their own.

Thick Sauce: Paragraphs are long and not uniform.

Spread Sauce: Paragraphs have typically the same length and cover the right amount of detail and information to complete the topic of the essay.

Image © sagasan, 2011. Used under license from Shutterstock, Inc.

But, paragraphs don't make up themselves without the little bits that melt together to make up a paragraph.

## Sentences Are Cheese

Sentence variety in an essay is just like melting cheese on pizza. The most common cheese on pizza, when it melts in the oven, brings once-individual strands of cheese together and becomes one united blissful unit on the entire pie. It is what is tasted first, from the beginning, and often what is mostly picked at on pizza. Idealized cheese on a pizza looks similar to:

So, there are kinds of cheeses that melt, like mozzarella, and others that don't have the same kind of moisture and protein that encourages that smooth melted look.

A cheese like feta will often stay the same shape after being baked.

Image © Foodpics, 2011. Used under license from Shutterstock, Inc.

Sentences are the cheese on the pizza. Because in order for sentences to have the mozzarella connection they need, they need to be complete and also have topic unification with the paragraph.

Imagine a pizza with 12 different cheeses on it.

Image © Gustavo Toledo, 2011. Used under license from Shutterstock, Inc.

When you bake that pizza, your sentences will be confusing because they lack structural unity in the essay. Short strands, chunks of tart, and half-melted center medallions of white do not help a pizza achieve its ideal pizza existence.

# PRACTICE

Describe the following cheeses with the type of sentence you think they might represent on a pizza.

Examples:

Feta Cheese: A short sentence that is out of place in the essay.

Goat Cheese:

Blue Cheese:

Parmesan:

Buffalo Mozzarella:

Asiago Cheese:

If only building a pizza were that essay. If only writing an essay was that easy. But, there are a plethora of other factors to consider, and it often depends on what you have available. If modern cuisine has shown humanity anything, it is that Californians might put too many things on pizzas that don't belong there, and the authentic traditional minimalist pie is not enough to satisfy the status quo. Just like an essay, all of the toppings you add into your essay can make it something tasty or nasty.

So, brainstorm with your class the top 10 pizza toppings that you all agree appear on a pizza:

1.

2.

3.

4.

5.

6.

7.

8.

9.

10.

Now, what are those extra parts of an essay that we might not have considered so far? We have the thesis statement, paragraphs, and sentences, which are all foundational, but how much more can we load up on the pizza?

Introductions / Conclusions / Topic Sentences / Hook Sentence / Diction / Proper Grammar and Spelling / Proper Formatting / Evidence and Support / Citations Page / Proofreading and Revision / Drafting / Organization / Punctuation

Now, as a class, assign the top 10 most important writing topics that you should include for your next assignment. What do you have to focus on?

| Ingredient List | Writing Attribute List |
| --- | --- |
|  |  |
|  |  |
|  |  |
|  |  |
|  |  |
|  |  |
|  |  |
|  |  |
|  |  |

Now, you get to make your own pizza!

On this pizza: Draw and then list the top 6 toppings that belong on your next Essay / Pizza.

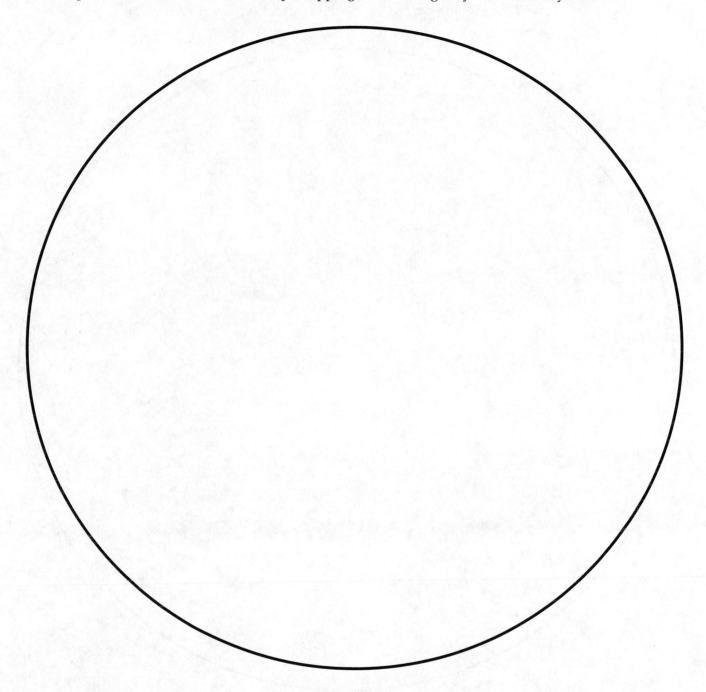

Now, on this pie, with a group of students, decide as a group which ingredients belong on this pie, but you can only choose four ingredients from your class list.

Write why you believe these ingredients are the most important factors of your essay.

How many groups have the same ingredients as your group? Tally them up!

The variance in essay ingredients is not just indicative of students' perceptions of what makes an ideal essay, because the pizza eater has the same problem as the student. Students, in their position as pizza makers, believe that the pizza they are serving their instructor is what was ordered. The order is the essay prompt. You believe you are baking the pizza the instructor wants. But it is possible that without specific lists on the order form, that each student has his or her own specific notions of what makes a strong thesis statement, how long the writing should be, and what kinds of writing style the instructor expects. This communication is not limited to the order form. Sometimes you can make an appointment to sit in a kitchen with the creator and eater to ensure you get what is expected.

Essays are pizzas. They vary as much as one another have been around as long, and both have so many interpretations that it is hard to pin down an all-encompassing definition.

But, this is exactly what analysis is.

**Analysis** is the means of looking at something as a whole by examining its parts.

You are now well versed in pizza pluralism. You know the parts—crust, sauce, cheese, and toppings. And that is analysis—looking at the specific parts of something and showing how the parts combine to define a whole.

Using this analogy, you can see how it is possible to engage in analysis of any topic. When constructing analysis, you are showing the parts you believe to be supportive of the overall point

# BUZZ WORDS FOR FOOD

Watch an hour of television during the day and keep track of all of the food-related commercials in that hour. Keep a list, noting what made them food related, who was in the commercial, and what kind of product was being sold.

| Name of Show: | Channel: | Time Watched: | Number of Food Commercials: |
|---|---|---|---|
|  |  |  |  |
|  |  |  |  |
|  |  |  |  |
|  |  |  |  |
|  |  |  |  |
|  |  |  |  |
|  |  |  |  |
|  |  |  |  |
|  |  |  |  |
|  |  |  |  |

## Respond

What is the link between your show and the types of food advertising shown?

How does this reflect on the viewing audience?

What were the major types of food ads?

Who was in the television show that you were watching, did it have a particular host or star?

Was there any product placement or advertising within the show you were watching?

**See the Course Website for a great video for behind the scenes of food on television!**

When you start to consider what makes up the parts of the whole, you can begin your journey to becoming a critical thinker. The ability for a college student to tear something down into its parts and make it a unified whole is essential. When you are looking at the everyday and realize that it is not just a whole pizza, but really made up of all of these intricate parts, it begins to open up your mind to seeing the possibility in any subject.

# WHERE DO YOU EAT? LOCAL FOOD ANALYSIS

In the previous chapter, you were asked to draw all of the local food opportunities within a short distance of your home. Whether this yielded a lot of choice is a byproduct of where you live. But consider your school location. What offers students choices to eat nearby? Are there fast food chains and cafeterias? What if you wanted something more unique? What if you wanted to support a small business? What would your options be if you were a vegetarian?

Depending on your needs as a consumer, your desires for particular food eateries shifts on almost a daily basis. If you were to consider the opportunities for eating places that were owned privately, how does this experience differ from when you are eating from a place that not only advertised to you since birth, but also can sponsor entire Olympic games within the blink of an eye?

# LOCALE

It is possible that while you are reading this book, right now, there is a burgeoning food scene happening around you. Down the street several food trucks are parked, offering their gourmet style; a blogger is trying a new place that specializes in food that you've never heard of; and recent American citizens are having a grand opening to share their cultural cuisine in the form of a new dining experience. Understanding the food history of your town is to also gain insight on the establishments that have been created through the local culture and the values that are still upheld.

Consider George Foster's analysis of the early New York food scene. Written in the mid-1800s, what are some of the conclusions we can draw from his analysis?

# THE EATING-HOUSES

George G. Foster

"Beef steak and taters vegetabes number twenty—Injinhard and sparrow grass number sixteen!" "Waiter! Waiter! Wa-Y-TER!" "Comingsir"—while the rascal's *going* as fast as he can! Is that beef killed for my porterhouse steak I ordered last week?" "Readynminisir, comingsir, dreklysir—twonsixprence, biledamand cabbage shillin, ricepudn sixpence, eithteenpence—at the barf you please—lobstaucensamming number four—yes sir!" Imagine a continuous stream of such sounds as these, about the size of the Croton river, flowing through the banks of clattering plates and clashing knives and forks, perfumed with the steam from a mammoth kitchen, roasting, boiling, baking, frying, beneath the floor—crowds of animals with a pair of jaws apiece, wagging in emulation of the one wielded with such terrific effect by R' LRNM —and the thermometer which has become ashamed of itself and hides away behind a mountain of hats in the corer, melting up by *degrees* to boiling heat—and you will have some notion of a New York eating-house. We once undertook to count these establishments in the lower part of the City, but got surfeited on the smell of fried grease before we got half through the first street, and were obliged to go home in a cab. We believe, however, that there can't be less than a hundred of them within half a mile of the Exchange. They are too important a "slice" of New York to be overlooked, and strangers who stop curiosity-hunting after they have climbed the big clock-case at the head of Wall-street, haven't seen half the sights.

A New York eating-house at high tide is a scene which would well repay the labors of an antiquarian or a panoramist, if its spirit and details could be but half preserved. Everything is done differently in New York from anywhere else—but in eating the difference is more striking than in any other branch of human cconomy. A thorough-bred diner-down-town will look at a bill of fare, order his dinner, bolt it and himself, and be engaged in putting off a lot of goods upon a greenhorn, while you are getting your napkin fixed over your nankeens (we think the cotton article preferable) and deciding whether you will take ox-tail or mock-turtle. A rgular down-towner surveys the kitchen with his nose as he comes up-stairs-selects his dish by intuition, and swallows it by steam and the electro-galvanic battery. As to digesting it, that is none of his business. He has paid all liabilities to his stomach, and that is all he knows or cares about the matter. The stomach must manage its own affairs—he is not in that "line".

Not less than thirty thousand persons engaged in mercantile or financial affairs, dine at eating-houses every day. The work commences punctually at twelve; and from that hour until htree or four the havoc is immense and incessant. Taylor at Buena Vista was nothing to it. They sweep every thing—not a fragment is left. The fare is generally bad enough—not nearly equal to that which the cook at the Home above Bleecker saves for the beggars, (generally her own thirteen cousins, "just come over.") It is really wonderful how men of refined tastes and pampered habits, who at home are as fastidious as luxury and a delicate appetite can make them, find it in their hearts—or stomachs either—to gorge such disgusting masses of stringy meat and tepid vegetables, and to go about their business again under the fond delusion that they have dined. But "custom," they say, does wonders; and it seems that the fear of losing it makes our merchant-princes willing to put up with and put down warm swill in lieu of soup, perspiring joints for delicate *entrees*, and corn meal and molasses instead of *meringues a la crème a la rose*.

There are three distinct classes of eating-houses, and each has its model or type. Linnaeus would probably classify them as Sweenyorum, Browniverous, and Delmonican. The sweenyorum is but an extension downward of the Browniverous, which we have already described. The chief difference to be noted between the two is, that while at Brown's the waiters *actually* do pass by you within hail now and then, at Sweeney's no such phenomenon ever by any possibility occurs. The room is laid out like the floor of a church, with tables and benches for four, in place of pews. Along the aisles (of Greece, if you judge by the smell) are ranged at "stated" intervals, the attentive waiters, who receive the dishes, small plate sixpence, large plate shillin, as they are cut off by the man at the helm, and distribute them on either side, with surprising dexterity and precision. Sometimes a nice bit of rosegoose, tender, may be seen flying down the aisle, without its original wings, followed closely in playful sport by a small plate bilebeef, vegetables, until both arrive at their destination; when goose leaps lightly in front of a poet of the Sunday press, who ordered it probably through a commendable preference for a brother of the quill; while the fat and lazy beef dumps itself down with perfect resignation before the "monstrous jaws" of one of the b'hoys, who has just come from a fire in 49th-street, and is hungry, *some!*

At Brown's we get a bill of fare, with the "extras" all honestly marked off and priced at the margin. But at Sweeney's we save our sixpence and dispense with superfluities. The bill of fare is delivered by a man at the door, regularly engaged for that purpose, and is follows:

Biledlamancapersors.

Rosebeefrosegoorosemuttonantaters—

Biledamancabbage, vegetables—

Walkinsirtakaseatsir.

This is certainly clear and distinct as General Taylor's political opinions, and does away with a great deal of lying in print, to which bills of fare as well as newspapers are too much addicted. The Sweeney, or sixpenny cut, is frequented by a more diversified set of customers than either of the others. It is not impossible to see, here, Professor Bush dining cheek-by-jowl with a hod-man off duty, nor to find a blackleg from Park-row seated opposite the police-officer whose manifest destiny it will be one of these days to take him to quod—unless he should happen to have money enough about him to pay for being let go. The editor, the author, the young lawyer, the publisher, the ice-cream man round the corner, the poor physician on his way to patients who don't pay, the young student of divinity learning humility at six shillings a week; the journeyman printer on a batter, and afraid to go home to his wife before he gets sober; in short, all classes who go to make up the great middle stripe of population, concentrate and commingel at Sweeney's. Yet all these varied elements never effervesce into any thing in the slightest degree resembling a disturbance; for eating is a serious business—especially when you have but sixpiece and no idea whether the next one has been coined.

It is true that Sweeney's "is emphatically a sixpenny eating-house"—but you must take care what you are about, or you may as well have dined at the Astor. —Unless you know how it is done, you will be nicely done yourself. If you indulge in a second piece of bread, a pickle, a bit of cheese, &c., &c., your bill will be summed up to you something after this fashion:—"Clamsoup sixpnce, rosebeef large, shilln, roastchikn eighteen, extra bread three, butter sixpnce, pickle sixpnce, pudn sixpnce, cheese three, clared (logwood and water alumized) two shilln—seven shilln." If you wish to dine cheaply, be contented with a cheap dinner. Call simply for a small plate of roast beef mixed, (this means mashed turnips and potatoes in equal quantities.) After you have eaten this frugal dish, —and it is as much as any one really needs for dinner,—you may send for "bread, hard," drink a tumbler of cool Croton, pay one shilling for the whole, and go about your business like a refreshed and sensible man.

There is still another class of eating-houses, which deserve honorable mention—the take and coffee shops, of which "Butter-cake Dick's" is a favorable sample,—The chief merit of these etablishments is that they are kept open all night, and that hungry Editors or belated idlers can get a plate of biscuits with a lump of butter in the belly for three cents, and a cup of coffee for as much more—or he can regale himself on pumpkin pie at four cents the quarter-section, with a cup of Croton, fresh from the hydrant, gratis. The principal supporters of these luxurious establishments, however, are the firemen and the upper circles of the newsboys, who have made a good business during the day, or have succeeded in pummeling some smaller boy and taking his pennies from him. Here, ranged on wooden benches, the butter-cakes and coffee and coffee spread ostentatiously before them, and their intelligent faces supported in the crotch of their joined hands, these autocrats of the press, and the b'hoys, discuss the grave questions as to whether Fourteen was at the fire in Front-street first, or whether it is all gas. Here also are decided in advance the relative merits and speed of the boats entered for the next regatta, and points of great pith and moment in the science of the Ring are definitively settled. As midnight comes and passes, the firemen, those children of the dark, gather from unimaginable places, and soon a panorama of red shirts and brown faces lines the walls and fills the whole area of the little cellar. They are generally far more moderate than politicians and less noisy than gentlemen. At the first tingle of the fire-bell they leap like crouching greyhounds, and are in an instant darting through the street towards their repective engine-houses—whence they emerge dragging their ponderous machines behind them, ready to work like Titans all night and all day, exposing themselves to every peril of life and limb, and performing incredible feats of daring strength, to save the property of people who know nothing about them, care nothing for them, and perhaps will scarcely take the trouble to thank them.

But of all this by iteself. The type of eating-house of which we have not spoken is the expensive and aristocratic *restaurant* of which Delmonico's is the only complete specimen in the United States—and this, we have it on the authority of travelled epictures, is equal in every respect, in its appointments and attendance as well as the quality and execution of its dishes, to any similar establishment in Paris itself. We have not left ourselves room in this number to speak in detail of this famous *restaurant*, nor of its *habitués*. It will deserves, however, a separate notice; and a look through its well-filled yet not crowded saloons, and into its admirable *cuisine* will enable us to pass an hour very profitably—besides obtaining a dinner which, as a work of art, ranks with a picture by Huntingdon, a poem by Willis, or a statue by Powers—a dinner which is not merely a quantity of food deposited in the stomach, but is in every sense and all to the senses a great work of art.

# WHERE'S THE MEAT?

Michelle Stonis

Whether you are cooking a steak or analyzing a source, you need the appropriate tools to get to the "meat," or the core, of the task at hand. A goal of analysis is to discover knowledge and meaning through thoughtful examination of a source. There are various methods you can employ to analyze sources, which are materials from which information is gleaned and meanings are constructed.[1] For your writing class, a source may be a nineteenth-century newspaper column or a squishy fruit on your plate. Below is a basic recipe for analyzing a source for a writing assignment. Remember, just like cooking, some of these ingredients may or may not apply to what your instructor is asking you to create, so check with your "head chef" before preparing your master creation.

# DO YOUR PREP WORK

An assignment's directions is your recipe for success. Know what is being asked of you and what product you are expected to create. What is the purpose of the assignment, and why are you being provided the source? Are you expected to replicate its style? Did your instructor want you to learn about a particular food culture? Were you to evaluate the source based on its writing method or prose? Just like preparing a cup of coffee, you need to know what to put into the brew in order to get the desired outcome. It is futile for both instructor and student alike if an essay on proper food preparation techniques is drafted for an assignment that is supposed to be about an author's writing style during the nineteenth century.

## Get Your Tools Ready

Keeping the assignment directions or desired outcome in mind, gather your tools in preparation to write. Do you need a source for comparison? Then a perusal of your local newspaper's food reviews may be necessary. Are you expected to learn the historical background of a location or the etymology of a particular food name? If so, a trip to your campus library or online research may be in order. Will you need to do any first-hand taste testing at a local eatery, or write multiple drafts of your essay before the specific due date? It sounds like some reservations, both at a restaurant and on your calendar, are required. Getting your tools ready is equivalent to putting all of a recipe's necessary ingredients on the counter; you are now ready to get cooking!

## Pass the Salt

As salt seasons food, so too will your analysis will flavor your work. You want to make sure you have the appropriate approach for the assignment at hand. Think of various ways of measuring salt as the approach you will take to analyzing your source, whether you need a bag of salt or just a dash. It would be useless to do a close contextual reading of a source if you are being asked to give a biography of the source's author. Various humanities disciplines have their own methods to apply to identify, analyze, and decipher meaning from a source. However, the focus of your class is primarily on the writing aspect of the assignment, not the exact professional method you are using to analyze the assigned topic. Regardless of the academic discipline, critical and analytical thinking skills are required to form a strong basis of knowledge built upon reason and evidence.

There are three basic ways in which you can approach a source. Based on your writing prompt, evaluate which analytical approach you need to take in adding salt to your work:

---

[1] Martha Howell and Walter Prevenier, *From Reliable Sources: An Introduction to Historical Methods* (Ithaca: Cornell University Press, 2001), 19.

*The Cup:* Imagine yourself as the chef who is pouring an entire heaving cup of salt into a pot. You are standing back, holding the cup high in the air while pouring it into the crock below. This is equivalent to having taking a bird's-eye view of a source. While you may analyze individual parts at another time, the cup approach means you are taking a survey of the entire source at once. Using critical thinking skills to assess the source, you are looking for overall similarities and differences while assessing the general tone of the source. You aren't putting the salt grain by grain into the pot. Similarly, this approach is about taking a cursory look at the minutia of the source and focusing on the big pot, or the big picture, in front of you.

*The Tablespoon:* With a tablespoon in one hand and a butter knife in the other, you gingerly scoop out a precise amount of salt and level it out for a distinct measurement. You dump the spoonful into a bowl of unmixed batter. It is then that you realize that you have many tablespoon-sized mounds of spices sitting like mountains on top of sugar-and-butter plains. The tablespoon approach is equivalent to having a magnifying glass view of a source. You approach the source looking to analyze various parts, the spices, individually. You may compare and contrast them, but in general you are looking to dig a little deeper into what the source tells you about various separate events, words, topics, ideas, or themes. This approach is equivalent to choosing something being presented in the material and analyzing that aspect throughout the source.

*A Pinch:* The finest chefs, and perhaps those who watch The Food Network, know that taking a pinch of salt means that precise attention is being paid to limiting the scope of the mineral in the overall dish. Novice chefs also know that there is no precise measurement for a pinch. Each chef has slight leeway as to how much salt he or she wants to add. This is also true of using the pinch approach. This method means that each person may approach the source with a unique focus and thus construct a different conclusion. The pinch approach means one specific aspect of the source is being analyzed individually, most likely with the intention to combine it with a few other pieces of analysis to add to a larger work. This approach means instead of analyzing a published restaurant review as a whole, you may analyze the author's view of using pickles in a specific dish while another person analyzes the treatment of the employees. Focusing on pickles, you add your analysis of the critic's viewpoint about pickles to many other examples of pickle viewpoints in order to craft your master essay titled "Pickle Fickle: Why Pickles Don't Belong in Fine Dining Restaurants." Brick-by-brick, pickle-by-pickle, you would use detailed analysis about pickles from various sources to build your argument.

## Dinner Is Served

What do a chef and a writing student have in common? You both are creating something that will be consumed and possibly devoured by critics. Using critical thinking skills is a learned process, one that takes you from a passive observer to a curious explorer attempting to find and create meaning out of the discoveries in a source. Just like a muscle, your analytical abilities will grow by exercising them as you challenging yourself. As you write about food and the meanings you have created from analyzing sources, remember that you, like a recipe, are a work in progress than is being fine-tuned through every draft, every feedback comment, and every new discovery in the classroom. It is not only the realm of published food critics to discuss and analyze the food culture around us all. Similarly, you don't need to be a professional historian in order to notice and analyze the change your neighborhood's food culture over the years. Unless you want someone to chew the tough stuff for you, use your analytical thinking skills to dig into the written and edible sources all around you. Fullness of the belly and the mind are both very satisfying. Pass the salt and a source, please. Let's dig in!

It is important that you establish your own criteria for what is good and bad about a place you might eat at. Fill out the following rubric with a classmate. Come up with the criteria you would use for giving the establishment a highest, lowest, and middle ratings.

Name of Business: _____

Type of Business: _____

| Subject of Criticism | $$$$ | $$$ | $$ | $ |
|---|---|---|---|---|
| Cleanliness: | | | | |
| Food Quality: | | | | |
| Commercial Appeal: | | | | |
| Packaging / Vessel: | | | | |
| | | | | |
| | | | | |
| | | | | |
| | | | | |
| | | | | |

If you were going to compare or contrast this place/item with another, what would it be and why?

_____

_____

_____

_____

_____

_____

_____

Draw a cartoon about your experience with your topic.

| | | |
|---|---|---|
| | | |

# DIRECTIONAL ANALYSIS

Let's say you are going to be a food writer who analyzes local food establishments. There are a few guidelines you'll have to consider when you are presenting your analysis to your readers to ensure that they trust you as a food critic, but another responsibility you have is to ensure that your reader knows what to expect from your analysis. If you editor says, "write about a restaurant that has the best service," approaching this question using directional analysis requires you to consider the process, or direction, a restaurant is required to take in order to achieve "the best service." What are the guidelines for "service"?

If you say that the fictional restaurant in my example "Smred Smloster" has the worst service of any seaside crabby patty fryer, directional analysis would walk us through how this place fulfilled the criteria.

- Smred Smloster has a dirty foyer area with a bored looking sea captain for a host, who did not look up and say "Ahoy!" upon entering.
- Smred Smloster did not seat my party of 25 efficiently, causing the smallest minnows in my party to be cranky and unappreciative of their food.
- Smred Smloster's server brought the cold food hot, and the hot food cold. There was also a lack of apology when the oysters were never opened for the slurping.
- Smred Smloster put another table's drinks on my tab, and then proceeded to accuse me of hiding in the bathroom, when I was getting over the problematic shrimp they served me, instead of paying the bill.

In directional analysis, your support would show how Smred Smloster fulfills those particular attributes.

# INFORMATIVE ANALYSIS

Now flip it. Smred Smolster is a place that achieves happy family time successfully. You can inform your reader of your support piece by piece.

- Smred Smloster provides children with fish hooks and pliers for their pre-meal entertainment.
- Smred Smloster offered lessons at the table of how to decapitate crawfish and suck the brain juice.

- Smred Smloster gave our table a free dessert for having a birthday celebration, they did not sing, which was thoughtful for our guest, who thinks that is both embarrassing and lame.
- Smred Smloster servers handed us balloons and chocolate mints as we left, and asked us to fill out a survey about our experience. They insisted we could be the winners of $500 and that they would love to see us return when we won.

Image © Michelangelo Gratton, 2011. Used under license from Shutterstock, Inc.

The biggest goals to consider with Directional versus Informative Analysis is to ensure that the reader understands the whole thing you are writing about, the criteria you support it with, and the emphasis you place in organizing your information.

# WRITING RESTAURANT REVIEWS

Even if you do not have the desire to become the next Ruth Reichl, Anthony Bourdain, or Guy Fieri, what you learn from their experiences can impact how you approach your own review.

### How do you find a place to review?

Ask a friend or family member for a recommendation.

Look in your local mail for advertisements for smaller places with smaller advertising budgets.

Check out Twitter or social media with specific hashtags, #yum.

Seek out people who have jobs at local establishments.

Look for local food blogs.

Check out resources for local vendors who gather at flea markets or farmers markets.

Popular review websites like Foursquare, Yelp, or popular Facebook pages.

## What will be your criteria for analysis?

Image © ducu59us, 2011. Used under license from Shutter-stock, Inc.

Will you only be focused on the food?

Will you tell your reader about the atmosphere or ambiance?

What kind of service are you expecting?

What can you tell by looking at the outside? The menu? The walls?

What kinds of people work in the establishment?

What kind of people do you expect to patronize the place?

Being able to engage in background information before you visit your restaurant is not cheating; it is research. Know where you are going; understanding the history of the place makes your visit more educational and worthwhile. If you enter a restaurant, and there are pictures of famous people with the owner, why would the owner place them there? When you realize that the sole purpose of the business is to entice the customer to go there, how does the place you analyze achieve that?

# DISCUSS

Discuss with your classmates how you would react to this kind of eating experience. How would a rude and aggressive server push you over the edge? What about not having menu options and assuming you would like particular foods? What would you expect a meal like that to cost?

## Analyzing Images

**Kevin decided to go for the
vegetarian option on the menu**

Image © Barry Barnes, 2011. Used under license from Shutterstock, Inc.

**Write about it!**

**What does this cartoon say to you about food?**

**Draw your own cartoon about eating out – use only one sentence for description and let your cartoon do the work for setting up your analysis!**

## ASSIGNMENT 1:

What do you know about your favorite local eatery? Consider an eating establishment that is privately owned in your local area. Write an informative analysis of how that establishment came to fruition and who keeps it up and running. Interview the owner for the inside scoop, and spend time getting to know who works there. Learn as much as you can about the purpose of the food it serves and how it differentiates itself from anything in the surrounding areas.

## ASSIGNMENT 2:

Write a local food review using only establishments with no more than two locations within a reasonable distance from your school. Analyze the establishment with your criteria for what makes this place significant for the area that it resides in. How does that particular kind of eatery find success in the cultural location of the area it is in? Research the origins of the eatery and how it is associated with the local community. What makes this place significant in the community?

# VOCABULARY

**Analysis** – Looking at something as a whole by examining its parts.

**Informative Analysis** – Presenting bits of information in straightforward evidence-based fashion to show how they make up the whole subject.

**Directional Analysis** – Showing a particular side of information to confirm your slant on the whole subject.

**Critique** – Thoughtful examinations of evidence and estimation of value.

_____

_____

_____

_____

_____

# Manifestos and Arguments

Chapter

**4**

This is the story of a little boy named Owen and his mother, Mrs. Flavaflay.

Owen is five years old. He's smart as a whip, of average stature, and has a bit of spunk in him. Owen is lucky, because he gets to eat dinner with his family every night at the designated dinner table. Now, I know what you are thinking—not all families "eat together" these days, but Owen has been afforded a traditional nuclear family that ritually eats together for supper. In addition to eating with his immediate family, he also gets a healthy diet, free of additives and preservatives, and fresh, local, and nutritious. Owen eats a varied diet, prepared by his mother, who takes great pains to ensure a well-rounded diet.

Image © grynold, 2011. Used under license from Shutterstock, Inc.

As part of presenting a varied diet for Owen, green beans are a weekly side dish for the family. Sometimes the beans are canned; sometimes they are fresh. Owen is only given five beans, one for each year of his existence, and in order to earn "clean plate-er" status, thus ensuring delivery of a dessert, he must accomplish the task of finishing the allocated green beans. Mrs. Flavaflay prefers that this happen without complaining or whining. However, as she serves the plate to him, he immediately shifts in his seat, groans, and puts his hand on his chin in disappointment. Sometimes he'll immediately cry, and ask why no one likes him, because if they did, they would know that green beans were something he could not eat. Mrs. Flavaflay serves everyone's ration; everyone needs to eat his or her vegetables.

Owen resists and resents the green beans on his dinner plate. "But, I really don't like them. They make my stomach hurt after I eat them and then I feel like I need to lie down. I don't care about ice cream any more, these are disgusting." His beet red face streams tears—he couldn't get up from the table until he ate the green beans. He offers to eat them for breakfast in the morning so he can get up. He barters eating more chicken or starch, but Mrs. Flavaflay is unwavering in her desire to feed Owen vegetables.

"But, you need a serving of vegetables. Look at your little sister, she is eating them and growing right before your eyes. Just close your eyes and eat them fast. If you don't eat them, then we are going to tell your teacher tomorrow. How about that?" And she convinces with statistics. And relays the personal experience of her own vegetables that she disliked and how green beans were not the end of the world.

Please just flippin' eat it already!

Image © RetroClipArt, 2011. Used under license from Shutterstock, Inc.

Owen doesn't hear it. And then he picks one single green thread on his fork, his lips barely parting enough to tickle his tongue with its green end. His nose curls in disgust. He shoves it in his mouth, sobbing as he chews, coughing as he swallows. He cried as he drank his water, attempting to wash it down, the vile bean. His plate fills slowly first, with a single cough he gags, and the first puddle plops onto his plate. His bread is suddenly soggy, and before she could reach for the napkins, his entire plate is ruined, inedible, and a rejection. "See! I'm allergic to green beans!" Owen is excused to brush his teeth and calm down.

Image © artproem, 2011. Used under license from Shutterstock, Inc.

Image © artproem, 2011. Used under license from Shutterstock, Inc.

So, who had the manifesto, and who had the argument?

# ARGUMENT

Now, believe me when I tell you that the above green bean situation happens on a daily basis all over the world. Even right now, there is a mother over a stove trying to both please and nourish a baby at the same time. So, why is this an argument? The argument about food starts when you are being formed as a young person, and throughout your life, every meal is a testament to how you have argued with food.

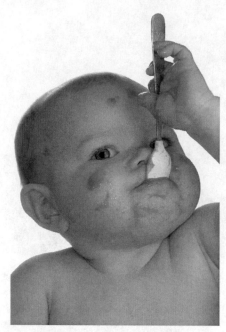

Image © Timothy Boomer, 2011. Used under license from Shutterstock, Inc.

When approaching a topic academically, argument is your chance to present information, reasons, support, and evidence. Often, arguments include a nod to the opposition, an understanding that there is another side to the presented argument, but it becomes obvious based on the presented argument that there are no real alternatives. This is the most often favored argument in academics.

Mrs. Flavaflay had numerous argumentative tactics, some she changed up with every table service that would include green beans. Each time, she presented a fact. But, just coming up with one or two facts is not really enough support despite their validity. "It's good for you." "You won't get dessert." "You have to stay there until you eat it all." These don't necessarily garner support; they are claims and demands by one side of the argument.

But Owen hates green beans. So much so that attempting to eat one would result in an immediate upheaval.

So, maybe if Mrs. Flavaflay presented her argument in a standard academic way, Owen would have been able to understand the ultimate point of her thesis.

**Thesis = Green beans are a healthy side dish for dinner.**

There are a few standard ways of presenting this type of argument.

## Socratic

This is the most familiar argument presentation, because it is the most standard form of presenting ideas in Western culture. Socrates passed this method down, which entails presenting a thesis, supporting it with points of evidence, and closing by restating a thesis.

How would you support the following thesis, and then restate it?

Thesis: Green beans are part of a nutritious and balanced dinner.

Supporting Point 1

Supporting Point 2

Supporting Point 3

Restated Thesis:

## Toulmin

Stephen Toulmin, an English logician, presented argument in a precise order to include the following elements:

Claim – The thesis that you want the reader to accept.

Grounds – The evidence that you want the reader to consider for why he or she should accept the Claim.

Warrant – How the Grounds are connected to the Claim.

Backing – The additional support for the argument.

Qualifier – Shows the strength of the claim.

Rebuttal – The point that shows that other side has been considered.

So, if Mrs. Flavaflay was presenting her green bean argument to Owen, she might lay it out like this:

Claim – All members of the family are required to eat their green beans.

Grounds – For consecutive years, the family has incorporated green beans into the diet; Owen has been exposed since infancy.

Warrant – Since Owen has been exposed to green beans since the introduction of solid food, he should continue to engage in eating green beans like the rest of his family.

Backing – There are no known green bean allergies within his bloodline, nor has he been diagnosed with a green bean allergy.

Qualifier – Most of the time, after eating green beans, he does not throw up on his plate.

Rebuttal – Although he would prefer other vegetables, such as lima beans, he is not in a position to make dinner decisions.

Now, at the end of Mrs. Flavaflay's Toulmin argument, you might be feeling for the kid. I mean, he might have been willing to eat another kind of vegetable; surely, making two vegetables would be a reasonable to accommodate Owen's picky palate. If Owen were going to present his own Toulmin argument, how would he incorporate all of these aspects his argument?

Claim -

Grounds -

Warrant -

Backing -

Qualifier -

Rebuttal -

## Rogerian

Mrs. Flavaflay could have been on Owen's level. She could have screamed, hollered, threatened bodily harm, held his nose, and shoved a bean in. But, Rogerian argument is about acknowledging the common ground that the argument holds between both sides, not ramming the argument down a metaphorical throat.

So, while the thesis for Mrs. Flavaflay is:

Green beans are a nutritious side dish and often a fixture in Mrs. Flavaflay's cooking cycle for her family.

The common ground for Owen could be:

A permanent substitution for his green beans would limit complaints about eating the vegetable served.

But, why would Mrs. Flavaflay go along with that? Finding common ground is an important aspect of presenting argument, but it requires the writer to not only consider the alternative aspect, but address it as well.

Why wouldn't Mrs. Flavaflay want to give into Owen's rebuttal? Provide five reasons:

1.

2.

3.

4.

5.

Now, create an outline for a Rogerian-style argument for your own commonplace food argument. Maybe you get into it with a local barista about how hot your latte is, or your Mom over what kind of milk she buys, or your significant other, who knows that you dislike mushrooms on pizza. Outline the thesis, and include opposing supporting points.

Thesis –

Supporting Point A1 –

Supporting Point A2 –

Supporting Point B1 –

Supporting Point B2 –

What would the person on the other side of your argument have to say about your ability and desire to find common ground? Share your argument with a classmate, and see if he or she would be won over by your side of the food argument.

# MANIFESTOS

The Oxford English Dictionary describes the word *Manifesto* in two ways.

1. A public declaration, written or spoken by someone who is in a status position.

2. A proof, a piece of evidence.

While the later entry is considered an obsolete usage of the word, the fact is that a manifesto relies heavily on the writers' ability to show evidence.

Are green beans good or bad?

Owen had a manifesto about green beans. He declared his disdain, his disregard, and the plethora of other dis-words that showed his distaste for green beans. His evidence was his projection onto the table.

Writing a food manifesto is a lot like vomit. Manifestos are not about length; they are about word power and ferocity. The goal of the manifesto is to move the reader into your cause because your drive is so convincing about your topic. Like vomiting, which often feels like it is powerfully thrown out of our bodies, often passionate ideas come out in a similar fashion. No one likes the concertgoer who throws up on a bouncer; if you are going to hurl, keep it on the down low and use a trashcan in the bathroom. Similarly with a manifesto, if you are on a street corner spewing your feelings and beliefs, which alienate the receiver, instead of creating something moving, the creation is abysmal and awkward. But when you construct and craft your message so it is controlled, emotive, and powerful, you open up the opportunity for the reader to accept your ideas. The only way that a manifesto becomes less like vomit is when, after the reader is finished reading, instead of feeling sick, he or she feels empowered and ready for action.

Have you ever read someone else's declaration, and been moved by it?

As a class, come up with a list of 10 different ways of declaring or manifesting an idea or belief –

1.

2.

3.

4.

5.

6.

7.

8.

9.

10.

Food manifestos often come from highly regarded people in the food writing circle:

Michael Pollan

Eric Schlosser

Alice Waters

Wendell Berry

Anthony Bourdain

Julia Child

Craig Claiborne

M.F.K. Fisher

Harold Mcgee

Jacques Pepin

Gordon Ramsey

Michael Ruhlman

Ruth Reichl

Who are these people? Do you recognize any of the names? Do you associate any of these names with ideas about food food? This is very similar to when you are using sources or an academic essay. Take, for instance, *The Art of Simple Food* by Alice Waters. Why would she have anything to say about food, let alone its being simple? From the start of her cookbook, she explains to the readers who she is, where she came from, and why this cookbook is important for the reader. She writes, "Good cooking is no mystery. You don't need years of culinary training, or rare and costly foodstuffs, or an encyclopedic knowledge of world cuisines. You need only your own five senses" (4).

What are Alice Waters' feelings about food?

"Food should never be taken for granted" (7).

All of these people have established careers in food writing, each spending decades and years studying and considering the ideas that have just been foisted upon you in this class. Many students may not have ventured into food in this way to feel like they have any room to say anything about their participation in their food system. But, the truth is that everyone does vote for the food issues they choose to ignore, not care about, or pretend do not exist with each bit they take from their fork. No one is immune from having to answer the question, "Where did your food come from and why do you eat it in the way you do?"

Develop topics with your classmates. What kinds of food issues do you think are important?

1.

2.

3.

4.

5.

6.

7.

8.

9.

10.

"manifesto." Oxford

# THE DAILY EATING DILEMMA

How do you know how many times to eat in a day? Do you listen to your mom's advice? The Department of Agriculture? A specific diet? Do you abide by cultural customs that dictate your diet or eating times? Is there flexibility in this? Typically, Americans are used to associating our meal plan to include breakfast, lunch, and dinner. In the last 30 years, the prevalence of snack foods has increased, creating the need for one or two snacks to be built within the day. And what about the donut before bed, does that belong to an eating time? Bedtime snack? Does this always stay the same, no matter our age? Is it wrong to stray from the "three squares" mantra?

Now, draw a diagram that shows your daily nutritional value:

# WHAT THE EXPERTS SAY

What is a food expert, and what does he or she say about eating? (Refer to the list on pg. 73–74 or find your own!)

Stretch out your research skills and find a web-based opinion about food from someone who is an "expert." All sorts of people have things to say about food, however, so you can decide what kinds of qualifications work for you—a chef, a doctor, a holistic healer, someone with experience, someone with a Ph.D. Poke around the Internet and find an expert. Then, locate his or her thesis statement.

Expert's name:

Expert's web location:

Expert's thesis statement about food:

Why did you pick this expert?

What is the summary of his or her presented advice?

Does this fit within the context of how you practice eating?

How are the presented arguments similar and different? Things to consider: tone, word choice, examples, support, and ability for you to connect with his or her ideas

# OWEN'S MANIFESTO

Earlier we compared a manifesto to vomit. It is also a comparison to be made because often, when writing about food, refuse becomes part of the equation The rejection of food is symbolic on many levels. When Owen is asked, only a few years beyond his age in the story, he still insists that he will weasel out of eating his green beans, sharing them with a sibling or passing basset hound, and throwing bigger attitude and bigger words at Mrs. Flavaflay. It may take years for him to come to terms with eating them, or he may be scarred forever and never again admit that he likes green beans. When discussing your own emotions about food, it is important to consider how the reader will accept your evidence.

# TAKE A PICTURE, IT WILL LAST LONGER

When you are discussing your own ideas and beliefs about the food you eat, you might need to paint a picture of what kind of situation is not ideal and what is the ideal your manifesto is aiming for.

Consider the word CAFO from Chapter 2. What if publishing images of CAFOs was an illegal act? Would you agree with this? Is this a free speech issue? Is there any point for the public to see pictures of CAFOs? Currently, some states are passing laws to prohibit this type of photography. How does our access to these images change our ideas about what it means to be an animal produced for food?

THIS OR THAT?

Image © Richard Thornton, 2011. Used under license from Shutterstock, Inc.

Image © 1000 Words, 2011. Used under license from Shutterstock, Inc.

## ASSIGNMENT 1

Think of a food choice, eating a specific kind of meat, drinking a type of drink, or engaging in any kind of food decision. Organize your essay using the Rogerian structure. Answer the question, What is the better choice for consumers? This or that? Be sure you support both sides with academic research!

## ASSIGNMENT 2

What topic, related to food, do you really care about? Do you think "good" food is a right? Are you anti-meat eating? Do you believe school lunches are defunct? Decide what you care about and take a stand in your food manifesto, be prepared to state your desire as well as suggest solutions for your reader to join in with you.

Watch:

Check out Jamie Oliver" Ted Award Acceptance speech on YouTube His speech is his Food Manifesto, in which he shows why he is passionate about students eating a healthy lunch.

<www.youtube.com/watch?v=jIwrV5e6fMY&feature=player_embedded>

# VOCABULARY

**Socratic Argument** – Presenting a thesis, using supporting points, and then restating the thesis.

**Toulmin Argument** – An argument that starts with what you want the reader to agree with and shows a systematic development of support.

**Claim** – The thesis that you want the reader to accept.

**Grounds** – The evidence that you want the reader to consider for why he or she should accept the Claim.

**Warrant** – How the Grounds are connected to the Claim.

**Backing** – The additional support for the argument.

**Qualifier** – Shows the strength of the claim.

**Rebuttal** – The point that shows that other side has been considered.

**Rogerian Argument** – Presenting an argument while giving an equal representation of the opposing argument.

**Manifesto** – A passionate message about something you want to happen or see changed.

_____

_____

_____

_____

_____

_____

_____

_____

_____

# REFERENCES:

www.oed.com.mms02.cerritos.edu:2048/view/Entry/113499?rskey=DyXOMT&result=1#eid   (OED: Manifesto)

# PART 2

# LET IT RISE AND THEN PUNCH IT IN THE MIDDLE

# Finding the Origin of Your Food

With the array of cable television shows and Internet feeds telling consumers where to eat and what to buy, there has been a recent transformation in the American *zeitgeist* of eating that has created the buzz of "eating local." It just so happens that I hail from the magical world of Anaheim, California, home of the original Disneyland Theme Park. Growing up in this area, I was never interested in what kind of foods were offered to me. There was a popular burger chain across the street from my high school, and another on the way home. But, when I was eating my grandmother's cooking, I believed I was getting the best from Mexico, in Anaheim. When we are young, we often accept the food that is given to us, it is passed down to us, and we absorb it as a part of who we are. Because of this, I grew up eating homemade tacos, tamales, and *albondiagas* soup.

If you are confused by my last name and my childhood "good eats," I can assure you that I am able to talk about tamales. My grandmother was born in 1930 to Mexican immigrants. My great-grandparents first settled in Central Coast of California, working at the grape and almond orchards with their families. My grandmother went to a local high school, one of only several students who were tanner than the rest. She told me it was a struggle to fit in, but she had her family and that helped her through it. Shortly after graduating, she married my grandfather, a white guy. They moved down to Orange County, where the jobs were popping up, and they settled in Anaheim.

She showed me her Mexican food, encouraging me to be proud to be part of a long tradition of food. She cherished her mortar and pestle, but never used it to make tortillas or grind anything. She ranted about the long laborious process of making tamales, but purchased her *masa* premade at a local *mexicatessan*. Her enchiladas contained mild cheddar cheese, she wouldn't think of using fresh *contija* or *queso fresco*; when I ordered *albondigas* for the first time in a restaurant, it looked nothing like what she had shown me in her kitchen.

Was I lied to? Was she lied to? How did the way she thought of Mexican food change over time? She told me stories about how the *gringos* at her work loved her tamales, but her mother would not be happy about the store-bought *masa*. Like many people, when we think about the origins of food, we have to realize that our own context for food is limited. My grandmother does not have the same idea about "Mexican Food" as the local Peruvian restaurant or the *Oaxacan taqueria*. Just like defining food, when we think about the origin of food, it is important to understand how a food fits in its context. All foods have a story, or tradition, a trend, or a symbolism; it just depends on who is telling those stories.

# WHERE DOES YOUR FOOD COME FROM?

Remember my grandmother's *masa*? Her favorite store to get it at is called *"Stanton Mexicatessen."* It is a "hole-in-the-wall" in the city of Stanton, which is next to Anaheim; they sell other things she needed for tamales, such as dried *pasilla* chilies and corn husks. She would buy the pork shoulder from the local major chain grocery store, as well as the canned chicken broth and canned black olives.

Despite the fact that she had addresses for the locations for all of the ingredients for her Christmas specialty, it is close to impossible to really know for sure where all of the ingredients *really* came from. Each ingredient comes from a complicated web of jet planes, trains, many trucks, and companies that are in charge of the basic commodities that people purchase on a daily basis. Where was the corn grown? Where did the farmer get the seeds?

When we start thinking about how hidden the world of where our food comes from is, we enter into a conversation about how we define the origin of our food, and that can shift what we find acceptable and what we do not.

# DINING OUTSIDE YOUR COMFORT ZONE

Humans are habit makers. Unless you go out of your way to introduce new foods, people often purchase the same food over and over again. Some people eat the same meal, on the same day each week, for years. Part of finding the origin of your food is to see what is accessible around you. Across America there are bubbles of nice-looking storefront developments that boast the trendiest food chains. Finding places that are truly owned privately and serving something that would be homemade, made the long way, or from a cookbook in another language, takes effort on the part of the eater. In Chapter 3: Analyzing Food, we talked about finding a local eatery and using analysis techniques to establish criteria for what is good about it and likewise see how the eatery impacts the surrounding area. Eating outside your comfort zone has a similar effect.

The box below represents your city. In your city, how many international eateries can you find? How many different kinds of cuisines are offered in your neck of the woods? Find one of each style eatery and list them below.

1.
2.
3.
4.
5.
6.
7.
8.
9.
10.

**Respond:** Do you eat foods that you are used to, or do you try to stretch your diet imagination? How do you feel about the access to multiple cuisines you have around you, and what improvements or cuisines are missing?

## THIS LAND IS MY LAND

For this idea to work, we cannot be flying to Hawaii. Imagine you are on an airplane; you are sitting at the window seat because you have the entire row to yourself flying across America. When you look outside the window, you see an array of squares and rectangles that make up a patchwork quilt of neatly laid lines, busy boxes, and lightly exposed soil.

Image © Popkov, 2011. Used under license from Shutterstock, Inc.

**Directions:** If one of those squares were yours, what would you grow?

If one plot represented your ability to grow any kind of crops, what would you grow? Create a sketch plan for your farm, including plans for barn, equipment, home, vegetation, orchard, or any other designated space for your farm plan.

Image © Scott E. Feuer, 2011. Used under license from Shutterstock, Inc.

Now that you have decided what should be grown in your garden, are you sure that you can actually grow these items in your backyard? In gardening world, seeds are often sold according to the buyer's climate zone, with particular plants doing better in specific climates. Using the Internet, find out your climate zone and evaluate whether the seeds would grow in your garden.

**Respond:** Did any plants not work out for you? Which would be great choices? How would you change your garden according to your climate?

I have to admit that it is a regular fantasy of my own that one day I'll "Thoreau" it. Henry David Thoreau (1817–1862) is an American author, widely known for his book *Walden*, which was a reflection on a simpler, isolated America. For two years, Thoreau lived on his own accord in a cabin by himself. Part political stance, social experiment, and declaration for sustainable self-reliance, Thoreau had to literally sow his own oats in order to eat.

# BREAD

Henry David Thoreau

I learned from my two years' experience that it would cost incredibly little trouble to obtain one's necessary food, even in this latitude; that a man may use as simple a diet as the animals, and yet retain health and strength. I have made a satisfactory dinner, satisfactory on several accounts, simply off a dish of purslane (*Portulaca oleracea*) which I gathered in my cornfield, boiled and salted. I give the Latin on account of the savoriness of the trivial name. And pray what more can a reasonable man desire, in peaceful times, in ordinary noons, than a sufficient number of ears of green sweet-corn boiled, with the addition of salt? Even the little variety which I used was a yielding to the demands of appetite, and not of health. Yet men have come to such a pass that they frequently starve, not for want of necessaries, but for want of luxuries; and I know a good woman who thinks that her son lost his life because he took to drinking water only.

The reader will perceive that I am treating the subject rather from an economic than a dietetic point of view, and he will not venture to put my abstemiousness to the test unless he has a well-stocked larder.

Bread I at first made of pure Indian meal and salt, genuine hoe-cakes, which I baked before my fire out of doors on a shingle or the end of a stick of timber sawed off in building my house; but it was wont to get smoked and to have a piny flavor. I tried flour also; but have at last found a mixture of rye and Indian meal most convenient and agreeable. In cold weather it was no little amusement to bake several small loaves of this in succession, tending and turning them as carefully as an Egyptian his hatching eggs. They were a real cereal fruit which I ripened, and they had to my senses a fragrance like that of other noble fruits, which I kept in as long as possible by wrapping them in cloths. I made a study of the ancient and indispensable art of bread-making, consulting such authorities as offered, going back to the primitive days and first invention of the unleavened kind, when from the wildness of nuts and meats men first reached the mildness and refinement of this diet, and travelling gradually down in my studies through that accidental souring of the dough which, it is supposed, taught the leavening process, and through the various fermentations thereafter, till I came to "good, sweet, wholesome bread," the staff of life. Leaven, which some deem the soul of bread, the *spiritus* which fills its cellular tissue, which is religiously preserved like the vestal fire,—some precious bottle-full, I suppose, first brought over in the Mayflower, did the business for America, and its influence is still rising, swelling, spreading, in cerealian billows over the land,—this seed I regularly and faithfully procured from the village, till at length one morning I forgot the rules, and scalded my yeast; by which accident I discovered that even this was not indispensable,—for my discoveries were not by the synthetic but analytic process,—and I have gladly omitted it since, though most housewives earnestly assured me that safe and whole-some bread without yeast might not be, and elderly people prophesied a speedy decay of the vital forces. Yet I find it not to be an essential ingredient, and after going without it for a year am still in the land of the living; and I am glad to escape the trivialness of carrying a bottle-full in my pocket, which would sometimes pop and discharge its contents to my discomfiture. It is simpler and more respectable to omit it. Man is an animal who more than any other can adapt himself to all climates and circumstances. Neither did I put any sal soda, or other acid or alkali, into my bread. It would seem that I made it according to the recipe which Marcus Porcius Cato gave about two centuries before Christ. "Panem depsticium sic facito. Manus mortariumque bene lavato. Farinam in mortarium indito, aquæ paulatim addito, subigitoque pulchre. Ubi bene subegeris, defingito, coquitoque sub testu." Which I take to mean—"Make kneaded bread thus. Wash your hands and trough well. Put the meal into the trough, add water gradually, and knead it thoroughly. When you have kneaded it well, mould it, and bake it under a cover," that is, in a baking-kettle. Not a word about leaven. But I did not always use this staff of life. At one time, owing to the emptiness of my purse, I saw none of it for more than a month.

Every New Englander might easily raise all his own breadstuffs in this land of rye and Indian corn, and not depend on distant and fluctuating markets for them. Yet so far are we from simplicity and independence that, in Concord, fresh and sweet meal is rarely sold in the shops, and hominy and corn in a still coarser form are hardly used by any. For the most part the farmer gives to his cattle and hogs the grain of his own producing, and buys flour, which is at least no more wholesome, at a greater cost, at the store. I saw that I could easily raise my bushel or two of rye and Indian corn, for the former will grow on the poorest land, and the latter does not require the best, and grind them in a hand-mill, and so do without rice and pork; and if I must have some concentrated sweet, I found by experiment that I could make a very good molasses either of pumpkins or beets, and I knew that I needed only to set out a few maples to obtain it more easily still, and while these were growing I could use various substitutes beside those which I have named, "For," as the Forefathers sang.—

> "we can make liquor to sweeten our lips
> Of pumpkins and parsnips and walnut-tree chips."

Finally, as for salt, that grossest of groceries, to obtain this might be a fit occasion for a visit to the sea-shore, or, if I did without it altogether. I should probably drink the less water. I do not learn that the Indians ever troubled themselves to go after it.

Thus I could avoid all trade and barter, so far as my food was concerned, and having a shelter already, it would only remain to get clothing and fuel. The pantaloons which I now wear were woven in a farmer's family,—thank Heaven there is so much virtue still in man; for I think the fall from the farmer to the operative as great and memorable as that from the man to the farmer;—and in a new country fuel is an encumbrance. As for a habitat, if I were not permitted still to squat, I might purchase one acre at the same price for which the land I cultivated was sold—namely, eight dollars and eight cents. But as it was, I considered that I enhanced the value of the land by squatting on it.

There is a certain class of unbelievers who sometimes ask me such questions as, if I think that I can live on vegetable food alone; and to strike at the root of the matter at once,—for the root is faith,—I am accustomed to answer such, that I can live on board nails. If they cannot understand that, they cannot understand much that I have to say. For my part, I am glad to hear of experiments of this kind being tried; as that a young man tried for a fort-night to live on hard, raw corn on the ear, using his teeth for all mortar. The squirrel tribe tried the same and succeeded. The human race is interested in these experiments, though a few old women who are incapacitated for them, or who own their thirds in mills, may be alarmed.

# WATERMELONS

Henry David Thoreau

Watermelons. The first are ripe from August seventh to twenty-eighth (though the last is late), and they continue to ripen till they freeze; are in their prime in September.

John Josselyn, an old resident in New England, speaks of the watermelon as one of the plants "proper to the country." He says that it is "of a sad grass-green color, or more rightly sap green; with some yellowness admixed when ripe."

September is come with its profusion of large fruits. Melons and apples seem at once to feed my brain.

How differently we fare now from what we did in winter! We give the butcher no encouragement now, but invite him to take a walk in our garden.

I have no respect for those who cannot raise melons or who avoid them as unwholesome. They should be spending their third winter with Parry in the arctic regions. They seem to have taken in their provisions at the commencement of the cruise, I know now how many years ago, and they deserve to have a monument erected to them of the empty cans which held their preserved meats.

Our diet, like that of the birds, must answer to the season. This is the season of west-looking, watery fruits. In the dog-days we come near to sustaining our lives on watermelon juice alone, like those who have fevers. I know of no more agreeable and nutritious food at this season than bread and butter and melons, and you need not be afraid of eating too much of the latter.

When I am going a-berrying in my boat or other carriage. I frequently carry watermelons for drink. It is the most agreeable and refreshing wine in a convenient cask, and most easily kept cool. Carry these green bottles of wine. When you get to the field you put them in the shade or in water till you want them.

When at home, if you would cool a watermelon which has been lying in the sun, do not put it in water, which keeps the heat in, but cut it open and place it on a cellar bottom or in a draught of air in the shade.

There are various ways in which you can tell if a watermelon is ripe. If you have had your eye on the patch much from the first, and so know the history of each one and which was formed first, you may presume that those will ripen soonest. Or else you may incline to those which lie nearest to the center of the hill or root, as the oldest.

Next, the dull, dead color and want of bloom are as good signs as any. Some look green and livid, and have a very fog of bloom on them, like a mildew. These are as green as a leek through and through, and you'll find yourself in a pickle if you open one. Others have a dead dark-greenness, the circulations coming less rapid in their cuticles and their blooming period passed, and these you may safely bet on.

If the vine is quite lively, the death of the quirl at the root of the stem is almost a sure sign. Lest we should not discern it before, this is placed for a sign that there is redness and ripeness within. Of two, otherwise similar, take that which yields the lowest tone when struck with your knuckles, that is, which is hollowest. The old or ripe ones ring bass: the young, tenor or falsetto. Some use the violent method of pressing to hear if they crack within, but this is not to be allowed. Above all no tapping on the vine is to be tolerated, suggestive of a greediness which defeats its own purpose. It is very childish.

One man told me that he couldn't raise melons because his children *would cut them all up*. I think that he convicted himself out of his own mouth. It was evident that he could not raise children in the way they should go and was not fit to be the ruler of a country, according to Confucius's standard. I once, looking by a special providence through the blinds, saw one of his boys astride of my earliest watermelon, which grew near a broken paling, and brandishing a case-knife over it, but I instantly blowed him off with my voice before serious damage was done—and I made such an ado about it as convinced him that he was not in his father's dominions, at any rate. This melon, though it lost some of its bloom then, grew to be a remarkably large and sweet one, though it bore, to the last, a triangular scar of the tap which the thief had designed on it.

The farmer is obliged to hide his melon patch far away in the midst of his corn or potatoes. I sometimes stumble on it in my rambles. I see one today where the watermelons are intermixed with carrots in a carrot bed and so concealed by the general resemblance of the leaves at a little distance.

It is an old saying that you cannot carry two melons under one arm. Indeed, it is difficult to carry one far, it is so slippery. I remember hearing of a lady who had been to visit her friends in Lincoln, and when she was ready to return on foot, they made her the rather onerous present of a watermelon. With this under her arm she tript it glibly through the Walden Woods, which had a rather bad reputation for goblins and so on in those days. While the wood grew thicker and thicker, and the imaginary dangers greater, the melon did not grow any lighter, though frequently shifted from arm to arm; and at length, it may have been through the agency of one of those mischievous goblins, it slipt from under her arm, and in a moment lay in a dozen pieces in the middle of the Walden road. Quick as thought the trembling traveller gathered up the most luscious and lightest fragments with her handkerchief, and flew rather than ran with them to the peaceful streets of Concord.

If you have any watermelons left when the frosts come, you may put them into your cellar and keep them till Thanksgiving time. I have seen a large patch in the woods frozen quite hard, and when cracked open they had a very handsome crystalline look.

Watermelons, said to be unknown to the Greeks and Romans. It is said to be one of those fruits of Egypt which the Jewish people regretted in the desert under the name of *abbattichim*.

The English botanists may be said to know nothing about watermelons. The nearest that Gerarde gets to our watermelon is in his chapter on "Citrull Cucumbers," where he says, "The meat or pulp of Cucumer Citrill which is next unto the bark is eaten."

In Spence's *Anecdotes* it is said that Galileo used to compare Ariosto's *Orlando* to a melon field. "You may meet with a very good thing here and there in it, but the whole is of very little value." Montaigne says, quoting Aurelius Victor. "The emperor Dioclesian, having resigned his crown and retired to 'private life,' was some time after solicited to resume his charge, but he announced. 'You would not offer to persuade me to this, had you seen the fine condition of the trees I have planted in my orchard, and the fair melons I have sowed in my garden.' ' Gosse, in his *Letters from Alabama*, says of the watermelon. "I am not aware that it is known in England; I have never seen it exposed in the London markets," but it is abundant all over the United States; and in the South:

> The very negroes have their own melon "patches," as well as their peach orchards, and it is no small object of their ambition to raise earlier or finer specimens than their masters. . . . [It] may be considered as the best realization of the French princess's idea of "ice with the chill taken off." . . . A cart-load is brought home from the field nearly every evening, to supply the demand of the family for the next day; for during this torrid weather, very little business but the eating of watermelons is transacted. If a guest call, the first offering of friendship is a glass of cold water as soon as seated; then there is an immediate shout for watermelons, and each taking his own, several are destroyed before the knife is laid down. The ladies cut the hard part, near the rind, into stars, and other pretty shapes, which they candy as a conserve for winter.

"Bread": *Walden* (1854); "Watermelons": *Wild Fruits* (2000: written 1859–62)

**Respond:** If you were going to "Thoreau" it, what would your fears be? What would you look forward to? Do you think you feed yourself off your own land and enjoy the fruits of your labor?

# JUDGING FOOD BY ITS LABEL

In the film *Food Inc.*, the narrator, Michael Pollan, describes the notion of the "pastoral narrative." When we traverse through the grocery aisles, we are confronted by packaged foods that have colorful labels, highlighted words, and emphasized notions meant to encourage us to purchase those foods. Pollan introduces the idea of "pastoral" through packages of breakfast foods that display a country farm, happy hens on the egg carton, and the farmer with a crack of wheat on the block of cheese. These images are very powerful indeed. Consider the images below and write your response to what you think the label would be for a specific food, who would buy it, how much it would cost, and where in the store you might find it:

Image © vso, 2011. Used under license from Shutterstock, Inc.

What kind of food would this be on?   How much does the item cost?

What quality is the product?   What kind of store would it be in?

Who is the product intended for?

Image © Gonchar Vlad, 2011. Used under license from Shutterstock, Inc.

What kind of food would this be on?    How much does the item cost?

What quality is the product?    What kind of store would it be in?

Who is the product intended for?

Image © LHF Graphics, 2011. Used under license from Shutterstock, Inc.

What kind of food would this be on?    How much does the item cost?

What quality is the product?    What kind of store would it be in?

Who is the product intended for?

Image © Dinesan Pudussery, 2011. Used under license from Shutterstock, Inc.

What kind of food would this be on?    How much does the item cost?

What quality is the product?    What kind of store would it be in?

Who is the product intended for?

Image © montebasso, 2011. Used under license from Shutterstock, Inc.

What kind of food would this be on?    How much does the item cost?

What quality is the product?    What kind of store would it be in?

Who is the product intended for?

Image © ducu59us, 2011. Used under license from Shutterstock, Inc.

What kind of food would this be on?    What quality is the product?    Who is the product intended for?
How much does the item cost?    What kind of store would it be in?

Image © ducu59us, 2011. Used under license from Shutterstock, Inc.

What kind of food would this be on?    What quality is the product?    Who is the product intended for?
How much does the item cost?    What kind of store would it be in?

**Respond:** Find some familiar labels in your cupboard and refrigerator. Sketch them below and conduct the same analysis as above.

What kind of food would this be on?

What quality is the product?

Who is the product intended for?

How much does the item cost?

What kind of store would it be in?

# ACTIVITY: INTERVIEW SOMEONE ABOUT THE WAY IT USED TO BE

The way that people grocery shop is unique to their place and time in the world. In America, the expansion of major chain grocery retail outlets has crowded out smaller family-owned grocery businesses of the past. What would it be like to grocery shop in the 1920s, 1930s, 1940s, 1950s, or 1960s? Have things changed much in the aisles since 1970s? Find someone who is at least two decades older than you to find out how it "used to be."

Name:

Sex:

Age:

Where did you shop for food?

What kind of environment was the store?

Were you able to get anything fresh and immediate?

Were you able to purchase from a farmer?

Did you know any of the people slaughtering your food?

Was the food source part of a community?

Is this place still available for me to investigate?

# WIC MILK CAN I BUY?

When I was constructing this chapter, I decided that the two staples that most people can get the most obsessed with are milk and eggs. For me, this is a true story of understanding that sometimes when we think we are buying milk, we aren't just buying milk.

One day an eating baby appeared in my care. When I became responsible for feeding someone else, I began to obsess over purchasing the basic home staples that I never thought about before. Let's face it, pre-kids, a life of Cheetos, malt liquor, and cake mix is about standard for many college students, and when you are out on your own on for the first time, sometimes eating the whole gallon of ice cream isn't a bad idea. But, then, a baby came into my life. I'll admit, it is cruel the obsession that Mother Nature decrees on the parent–child relationship: Children come with an endless pressure to feed and please them (more on that in another chapter), but the pursuit of milk became my obsession. When I was at the store, I noticed flags on the milk racks that designated particular foods "WIC" approved. I asked the grocer about it; it was a food stamp program for pregnant mothers and children to make their lives easier to know which foods they could purchase with their coupons. While in line checking out, a woman was purchasing a vast amount of formula and had gallon jugs of milk, the cashier was going through hoops to charge her and fill out her forms, the people behind her were antsy for her transaction to end. The next time I went to the grocery store, I paid careful attention to which milks were approved and which were not. Organic milk was not going to fly up there. At $5.99 a gallon, it was the most expensive. The name brand milk labeled that the cows were not treated with growth hormones was not acceptable. The generic milk that is normally on special, 2 for $6, had pastel signs; pick them up WIC women! I asked the clerk how much the coupon voucher was good for with the milk, and for a gallon, the check was reimbursable for around the same price as the organic milk, yet the store would only sell the generic milk in exchange for the coupon.

Wait? What?

The store gets to regulate which milk the coupon is good for. The WIC mom has to take her chances with the hormone-infused milk?

Who gets what milk? Who gets to know what is really in her milk or where it comes from?

# ACTIVITY

Many food programs have different kinds of foods that they offer to their communities. What do you think about your local food program? Research a food assistance program near you such as a food bank, soup kitchen, co-op, school program, or government program and analyze the food it offers people. Where does this "free food" come from? Is it healthy? Is it of good quality? How do the patrons feel about getting it?

Image © Kuzma, 2011. Used under license from Shutterstock, Inc.

# WHERE IS MY MILK FROM?

Image © basketman23, 2011. Used under license from Shutterstock, Inc.

It turns out that all dairies are assigned a code that they stamp on their milk products so the consumer can find out where his or her milk comes from. At Whereismymilkfrom.com, consumers can see where their milk comes from.

But, wait! Before you look it up…how far do you think it comes from? Write down an estimate in miles here before you go look:_____

Draw a map from your house to where your milk is from:

What kind of product is it?

What is the dairy name?

How many miles is it from you?

Do you feel that this is far or close?

# MY EGGS!

The labels for chicken eggs are confusing. I denote chicken eggs because in some grocery stores, in a properly ethnically diverse community, it is possible to stumble upon quail or goose eggs. But, the run of the mill carton of chicken eggs is no laughing matter. We know the egg came from a chicken, but does it matter how the chicken lived before the egg popped out? Does that affect the egg when you end up cracking it open? There are specific guidelines to realize when considering the ideal chicken life.

Chickens like to scratch around dirt for grubs, bugs, food specs, and make chicken noises. I can attest the sound is unlike any other. A friend of mine has a small backyard flock, and it is enjoyable to hear

Image © Becky Stares, 2011. Used under license from Shutterstock, Inc.

them in the morning hours while we have coffee. They sound more melodic than our own cackling. The low cooing of hens is apparent when they are laying eggs, which when they are walking around, getting exercise, and eating a natural diet; they create egg yolks that are rich in Omega-3 fatty acids and often have deep color and tone.

But, some chickens don't get to gestate in this kind of environment. And while this picture doesn't make it look THAT bad, it's a far cry than the natural ideal habitat.

Image © Enrico Jose, 2011. Used under license from Shutterstock, Inc.

Refer to the term battery cage in Chapter 2: Defining Food.

The words on the egg carton mean something. A chicken that lays eggs "free-range" has no freedom, and a "cage-free" chicken can still have confinement. But, maybe the real truth to this matter is to test the eggs for yourself and see what you observe. We are what we eat, and chickens lay what they are treated with. It is getting easier to find truly cage-free eggs. Often the local farmer's market will carry some; of course, high-end grocery stores have them covered, and some even add the "organic" label.

It is important that the natural diet of a chicken is a scratch in a garden or compost pile and maybe a supplement of chicken feed. But, what is in chicken feed? Mostly corn, soybeans, or flax seeds, all of which can be genetically modified. A chicken that is "vegetarian fed" is confusing since chickens are omnivorous. Find the most "free" chicken eggs you can, even if it means you ask a friend with a backyard flock for a single egg. Then purchase eggs from a dollar store or without any specific packaging regarding the treatment of the chicken.

| | Free Egg | Caged Egg |
|---|---|---|
| Brand of eggs | | |
| Pictures on carton? | | |
| Specific labeling on carton? | | |
| Grade of egg? | | |
| Location of distributor | | |
| Location of chicken farm | | |
| Color of shell | | |
| Size of egg | | |
| Weight of egg (felt by hand) | | |
| Any imperfections or beauty marks? | | |
| How does it crack? | | |
| What does the white look like? | | |
| Is there any blood or altered coloring of the yolk? | | |
| What color is the yolk? | | |
| Is the yolk firm or soft while raw? | | |

Now, try frying it up and seeing if there is a difference in smell and taste! Note your observations on the following charts.

**Taste**

**Smell**

## ASSIGNMENT 1

Choose a food that you are familiar with because you eat it often, but really don't know much about where it came from. Do in-depth academic research on this item and discover as much as you can about it, where it comes from, who grew it, how it got to you, and the impact of your buying it. Reflect in your work on any alternatives that would be better for the environment, for your health, or a substitute that would be an improvement.

## ASSIGNMENT 2

Research the origin of your favorite childhood food. Analyze and evaluate the origin of your favorite dish so readers can recreate the dish themselves from your direction. Tell us your history of this item, where you first ate it, who made it for you, and if this is something that the original person can still prepare for you. Be sure you include instructions for preparations and specific ingredients. Include a recipe card and picture.

## ASSIGNMENT 3

Write a persuasive support letter for a local food program. Find a food program that you support and discover all you can about the type of help that it offers, what kinds of foods it has access to, and explain what this organization does to benefit the food community.

# VOCABULARY:

**Free Range** – Laying hens houses in indoor pens with a small door that gives access to a small patch of outdoors.

**Cage Free** – Laying hens that are not caged.

**Homogenized** – A process that evens out the fat molecules in milk.

**Pasteurized** – The cooking of milk to kill bacteria.

**Masa** – A ground corn mixture used in making tamales.

**Tamales** – Often served for Christmas in Latin American cultures. A filled corn husk with masa around many types of fillings. A laborious recipe, especially when made from scratch.

**Albondigas** – Meatball soup.

**Anaheim** – A city in Southern California, home of Disneyland.

**Orange County** – Between Los Angeles, San Diego, and Riverside County.

**Label** – The textual statement between a consumer and the product.

_____

_____

_____

_____

_____

_____

_____

_____

_____

_____

# Spinning Plates for the Children

## HOW IT WAS DONE

Grandma had stories that made my eyes widen. These were the stories of how it used to be and how she used to get things done. Simple things. When she was a teenager, she wanted to have tan-looking legs. She would drag tea bags over her legs, attempting to stain them. She told stories of waking up early to roll out tortillas for her father.

She would tell me about saving lemon peels from the garbage disposal and how to compost leftover food. She told me stories of saving foil during the Second World War, and chastised me if I used too many paper towels.

She grew her own food, as much as she could while working full time. While she was a grandmother, often with a grandbaby in the yard playing in the dirt, she would clip around and pick oranges with fervor, not allowing anything to go to waste.

She would give a lemon wedge to a baby, laughing at the pucker on its face when it struggled with its senses. Sometimes she would be angry and crack open a can of Budweiser. When she was really cooking up a storm, especially for a holiday, she was worried, concerned about everything coming out just right. Things had to happen a certain way. Making her red enchiladas was a standard practice on holidays, and the cheese had to be grated the hard way, with a block of cheddar and a box grater. Don't even bring up buying a bag of shredded cheese. "Why, are you lazy?"

My grandma doesn't have the ability to remember any of her recipes or ways anymore. Suffering from Alzheimer's, her words are a scrambled puzzle; she is frustrated when the faces in front of her do not understand her words anymore. I can't ask her how to make anything; all I have is the images and memories from my own eyes.

When you are a child, the people who are important to you leave their mark in more ways than the traditional genetic traits we inherit. What we see around us as representations of food, from the time we are young, has a large impact on how we view the world. People all over the world are brought up to savor food, waste food, prepare food, and pass on the traditions of food, but the ways that we do things make us who we are. Sometimes we have to grate life to work it out.

# HAVE YOU TRIED MY ENCHILADAS?

We shred the hard way
dominating the rusted silver
box grater with spiked sides
shaving orange curls.
Cool corn discs bubbling
the hat dance on
the pool of fat
tamed by wooden spoon.
Abuela rolled and twisted
missed a pit and
tucked black truth
under crispy edges,
tooth breaking pebbles doused
in eerie La Victoria red
sauce and secrets,
sopped and sweated
the cheese I grated.
She melted me instead,
raining roughly chopped scallions
onto my boiling skin.

[http://labelmelatin.com/wp-content/uploads/2011/03/HAve-you-tried-my-enchiladas-lyndsey-lefebvre.pdf]

**Respond:** Write about a childhood food that you feel a connection to. Describe your feelings about this food and constructor a poem or free write about this dish.

# LEARNING ABOUT FOOD

With the current rise of childhood obesity, there is much concern about the relationship between children and food. Some cities have banned toys in kids' value meals, and there are murmurs about reducing the advertisements that are heavily displayed during kids' television shows. With so many messages being sent to children about food, what do you think today's 3-year-old learns? How do children learn about food?

Consider the following images and construct the food plan for this child. Who buys his food? Is he a good eater, or is he picky? Based on the image, what do these children think about food? Think about demographics, social class, personality, and anything else you might analyze in the image.

Image © Serhiy Kobyakov, 2011. Used under license from Shutterstock, Inc.

What kind of food reality do these children have?

Image © Zurijeta, 2011. Used under license from Shutterstock, Inc.

What kind of food reality do these children have?

Image © Estelle, 2011. Used under license from Shutterstock, Inc.

What kind of food reality do these children have?

Image © Zurijeta, 2011. Used under license from Shutterstock, Inc.

What kind of food reality do these children have?

Image © Wallenrock, 2011. Used under license from Shutterstock, Inc.

What kind of food reality do these children have?

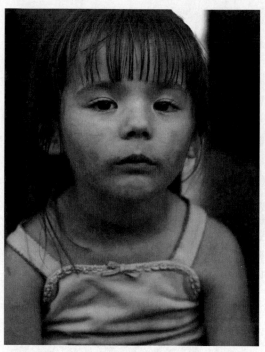

Image © jmatzick, 2011. Used under license from Shutterstock, Inc.

What kind of food reality do these children have?

Image © Zurijeta, 2011. Used under license from Shutterstock, Inc.

What kind of food reality do these children have?

Image © Larisa Lofitskaya, 2011. Used under license from Shutterstock, Inc.

What kind of food reality do these children have?

Image © Lucian Coman, 2011. Used under license from Shutterstock, Inc.

What kind of food reality do these children have?

# FOR HOMEWORK, GO WATCH TV

Image © dubassy, 2011. Used under license from Shutterstock, Inc.

Maybe it's been a while for you, but kid shows have been showing advertisements to children since the black-and-white days of *Howdy Doody*. Advertisements for breakfast cereal, beverages, and other processed foods have been pumping money into popular shows for decades. But, maybe it has been a while since you've looked at what kinds of foods are being offered to children while they watch television.

Select three shows, one that is for preschool children (3–5 years), one for kids (6–12), and one for teens (13–17). Record all food advertisements and include mentions of food within the context of the television show. Record the product with as much detail as possible (i.e., Mr. Tastee's Chocolate Chip Pancake on a Stick) as well as the way the ad is presented (i.e., Pancake gets stabbed by a stick and is eaten alive by child).

Preschool Show:

Channel:

Length of Show:

Date of Airing:

| Product | Advertisement |
|---------|---------------|
|         |               |
|         |               |
|         |               |
|         |               |
|         |               |
|         |               |
|         |               |

| Product | Advertisement |
|---------|---------------|
|         |               |
|         |               |
|         |               |
|         |               |
|         |               |
|         |               |
|         |               |

Kid Show:

Channel:

Length of Show:

Date of Airing:

| Product | Advertisement |
|---------|---------------|
|         |               |
|         |               |
|         |               |
|         |               |
|         |               |
|         |               |
|         |               |

| Product | Advertisement |
|---------|---------------|
|         |               |
|         |               |
|         |               |
|         |               |
|         |               |
|         |               |
|         |               |

Teen Show:

Channel:

Length of Show:

Date of Airing:

| Product | Advertisement |
|---------|---------------|
|         |               |
|         |               |
|         |               |
|         |               |
|         |               |
|         |               |
|         |               |

| Product | Advertisement |
|---------|---------------|
|         |               |
|         |               |
|         |               |
|         |               |
|         |               |
|         |               |
|         |               |

# RULES FOR EATING

Often the ways that eating traditions and customs are translated are through the uses of rules. These rules are often created as part of an etiquette system. Etiquette simply represents a set of rules or guidelines that govern a person's behavior. Etiquette can often vary depending on one's culture, age, economic status, or family life. Food etiquette, for instance, can vary widely from person to person.

Take this inventory and compare with your class. These rules can range from the food you put in your mouth to the way you lay a napkin on your lap. What kinds of rules are prevalent, popular, or popping out at you?

*List food rules you followed in elementary school.*

1.

2.

3.

4.

5.

*List food rules that you broke when you were young.*

1.

2.

3.

4.

5.

*List food rules that your family wants you to follow.*

1.

2.

3.

4.

5.

*List food rules that you have shared with other people.*

1.

2.

3.

4.

5.

*List food rules that were taught to you by an expert in nutrition.*

1.

2.

3.

4.

5.

*List food rules that were taught to you by a doctor or physician.*

1.

2.

3.

4.

5.

*List food rules that you have learned since the beginning of your adulthood.*

1.

2.

3.

4.

5.

*List food rules that you think are totally unreasonable.*

1.

2.

3.

4.

5.

**Respond:** Compare your answers with your fellow classmates and identify the variety of rules that people are taught about food. Create a class comparison and contrast, reflecting on rules that are common and others that are uncommon.

## Congratulations on YOUR new addition!

Let's just pretend for a moment that you have just given birth to a new baby. (If you happen to be male, just remember that a man has already given birth in this world, and it's pretending, just play along.) How do you feed a baby? No, like, when it first comes out of its vessel and is in this world with us. We all know that humans eat food, but what do you think is a typical "first food" for a baby?

What do babies eat? _____

There is much debate in the world of motherhood over how to feed an infant. When someone becomes responsible for someone else's sustenance, it can create an overwhelming desire to ensure that the baby is getting proper nutrition.

So, which is better, breast or bottle?

Image © Igor Stepovik, 2011. Used under license from Shutterstock, Inc.

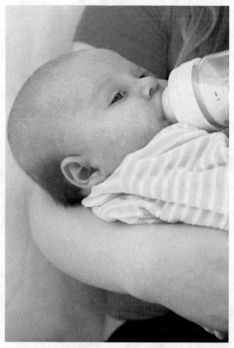

Image © Shchipkova Elena, 2011. Used under license from Shutterstock, Inc.

If you haven't been in this situation before, then this is an opportunity to look at this decision through an academic lens. Have you ever witnessed a mother breastfeeding her child? What kind of struggles may she encounter in public when her baby needs to eat? How does a breastfeeding mother make *you* feel?

Conduct preliminary research about the pros and cons of feeding a new baby.

Breastfeeding

Bottle Feeding

**Interview**: Talk to a new mom about her experience feeding her new baby. How is it easy, difficult, or challenging? Does she have concerns? Is there someone that she asks for help?

Discuss with the class how you would present an academic argument on this topic. How do your initial feelings toward the subject impact your ability to relay the information academically?

## ACTIVITY

Image © Teresa Kasprzycka, 2011. Used under license from Shutterstock, Inc.

Have you ever played the baby shower game with unmarked baby food jars? What's in there? Peas? Green Beans? Spinach? What kinds of foods are marketed to parents for emerging eaters? Check out the baby food aisle at your neighborhood grocery store and note what kinds of food products are sold for babies. Do these foods fall under the nutritional needs of an infant? How do we know?

## THE EDIBLE EDUCATION

**Research:** What are the requirements in your community for students to learn about food? Using the Internet and your best research skills, search for the curriculum standards for your locale. Often these are linked through websites for school districts or state department of education websites.

Elementary School Curriculum:

Junior High / Senior High Curriculum:

Do any schools in your area offer specific programs for kids who want to be involved with food?

It is the contention of several food activists that many of the heath challenges in America stem from the lack of connection between people and their food. One of the ways that activists have been promoting this idea is to encourage schools to incorporate community gardening on their school grounds or to allow students a more active role in the kitchen.

Check out the following websites about edible educations:

www.realschoolgardens.org

www.edibleschoolyard.org

www.jamieoliver.com/foundation/jamies-food-revolution

**Respond:** Based on these programs, what kinds of improvements would you like to see made in your own community?

# THE BELL RANG! IT'S LUNCH TIME!

Image © Suzanne Tucker, 2011. Used under license from Shutterstock, Inc.

During the first airing of the *Jamie Oliver Food Revolution*, which featured the quaint town of Huntington, West Virginia, Jamie surveyed a school cafeteria at lunchtime. He noticed not only the lunch that the school provided, but also surveyed the lunches that the children brought from home. Before we talk about the broader appeals of school lunches, let's first do an inventory of your experiences.

1. Describe your lunchtime in elementary school. Did you eat outside or inside? Did you have to sit with specific people? Were there any rules that needed to be followed?

2. Were there different rules for people who ate school lunch and people who at from home?

3. How much did a school lunch cost? Were some choices more expensive than others? Which ones cost more/less?

4. Which was more prevalent at your school, eating in the cafeteria or "brown bag"?

5. Do you remember any adults present during lunchtime? Did any adults eat with children? Were there any special occasions for student to interact with teachers during lunch?

6. Were your eating habits monitored by anyone? What would happen if you refused to eat your food?

One of the more eye-opening things Oliver concluded from his observation was that the lunches served by the school were equally as unhealthy as the lunches that parents were sending to school with their children. Students purchasing school lunch were allowed to buy many types of processed snack foods, and similarly, the kids he witnessed often brought lunches from home that included cans of soda and chips. When Oliver attempted to change the lunch policies of the school, he was met with opposition from many in the community. What about the children? What do you think kids want out of their lunchtime experience?

## Interview

Find three elementary school children and talk to them about their lunchtime experience. Ask them similar questions as you answered and inquire about their attitudes about food at school. Is it something they look forward to? Do they think they should have less time to eat and more time to play? How do they feel about the rules within their institution?

# LUNCHES ACROSS THE WORLD

Image © moriko, 2011. Used under license from Shutterstock, Inc.

In Japan, a child's lunch box is serious business. Whether the child eats the food that his or her mother packs can end up being a direct judgment on the abilities of the mother. This has led to a furthering popularity of the Bento Box, the infamous child's lunch with reflects not just nutrition, but novelty. Often shaped into animals and characters, Japanese sushi in kids' lunches resembles homemade works of art, rather than the Sloppy Joe style food American kids typically eat at the school cafeteria. What do kids in other countries find in their lunch box?

Image © mojito.mak[dog]gmail[dot]com, 2011. Used under license from Shutterstock, Inc.

Check out the "What's For School Lunch" blog for pictures sof school children around the world: http://whatsforschoollunch.blogspot.com

Use this space for taking notes on the countries that you are interested in:

| Country #1 | Country #2 | Country #3 |
|---|---|---|
| Describe Children / Setting - | Describe Children / Setting - | Describe Children / Setting - |
| Describe Food – | Describe Food – | Describe Food – |
| Describe Place Settings / Utensils – | Describe Place Settings / Utensils – | Describe Place Settings / Utensils – |

# KIDS WHO DON'T EAT

Despite the best efforts of every adult in a community, there are always possibilities for children to be hungry. It is not uncommon for the peasant-child to exist in our modern society. It is, however, in the maze of capitalist American culture, easier for the *have-nots* to become lost among the *haves*.

One night, Owen and I were having evening snuggle when HBO began to air a documentary titled, *The Motel Kids of Orange County*, which was filmed in the same areas of Anaheim in which I grew up, and the area I have been raising my own kids. I let Owen stay up late and we watched it together. There were kids who, due mostly to homelessness, were sometimes hungry, living in stressful situations, and enduring the rampant crime all around them, all in one of the wealthiest counties in California. The film showed various landmarks around us that Owen recognized, including hotels around that famous theme park. When the film was over, Owen had questions. Do the kids still live there? Where would they go to school if they had to move? Why do some kids have it so hard?

Living in a motel does not allow for the type of cooking environment that a standard kitchen would afford. How do you think your childhood would have been different if you had to grow up in one room with your family, perhaps without a stove or microwave at your disposal? Or further, it is possible this was your reality; what are some of the issues with food and residence that people might not realize?

Despite the frustration with these children being unable to participate in the traditional suburban "OC" childhood of beach days and barbeques, there are still members of the community who try to alleviate this issue. The Anaheim White House, one of the top restaurants in Anaheim Resort area, has been taking care of motel kids for several years. Executive Chef Bruno Serato has even accepted pasta donations from customers so that the establishment can help the underserved children in motels around the area.

**Respond:** Are there community organizations in your area that help with this problem? How do they help children in this situation? Do you have a local leader for this issue? Research for your area and find out what kind of support your local leader needs and write a promotional article for them. How can a cause like this attract more people to help?

Name: _____   Date: _____

# ASSIGNMENT 1

You have just been given the power to change your childhood elementary school's lunch program into your own inspired food program. What would students going to that school participate in? What would you ensure they learn, when would they learn it? Be sure you address how your school could raise revenue or save money for your changes and what kind of school leadership would be required to enact the changes you think should be made. Your ideas for change can be as little as adding or removing foods to and from the menu, to as grand as starting a school-run dairy farm. Use interviews as support for your changes.

# ASSIGNMENT 2

Consider the current school food policies of the USDA. Write a research paper that shows what the regulations are for school districts to follow. Write about this topic in its most current form, as the bill for funding school lunch programs has recently changed. Evaluate the requirements for school lunches with your personal experience and decide if you would listen to the guidelines, or if you want to work toward something different.

# VOCABULARY

**Food Etiquette –** A set of rules or guidelines that governs a person's behavior.

**USDA –** United States Department of Agriculture.

**Brown Bag –** School brought from home rather than purchased at school; named for the small brown paper bag that often acts as a lunch carrier for children.

**Motel Kids –** Children of homeless families who lack a permanent residence, and must rely on local motels for food and shelter.

_____

_____

_____

_____

_____

_____

# If You Cook, I'll Clean Up

Before we start this chapter, let's all ascertain one thing as a class. Without looking at other peoples answers, fill in the blank:

A woman's place is in the _____.

What did you put?

Image © RetroClipArt, 2011. Used under license from Shutterstock, Inc.

Is this the picture that comes to mind when we think about the placement of women in our homes?

# I DO AND I DON'T

This book will be released in the year 2014. As of that year, I will be married for a decade. This isn't about how much I love cooking for him, or how I hope my food is the backbone of our family. The reality is that regardless of whether one of us likes to cook is not relevant to the fact that we both need to eat and also feed our children, and that food will be the backbone, the foundation for how our family functions gastronomically that is passed on to future generations.

When we were trying to figure out who was best in the kitchen, there was a realization that our childhoods were different, and we became two separate food entities in the same house. As our children grow older, we have to consider what they will or will not eat, and then every holiday we have to remember which relative doesn't like a particular thing that the other side of the family believes is essential. Suddenly, food worlds collided, and at the end of it, we sometimes fight over the merits of spending more money on organic milk, whether the kids know the different between cow milk and almond milk, why garlic is his favorite despite the fact his mother hates it, and why I think sour cream can go with anything. The only ultimate agreement we have is the Cook–Cleanup Clause of our marriage. "If You Cook, I'll Clean It Up" became the mantra for deciding who was more tired to do one aspect of household duties. Do you want to cook, or do you want to clean it up? This is the way we solved our dinnertime marital problems, sometimes at breakfast, too. Why is it so important for equality in the modern marriage? But what if he didn't cooperate with me? What if his ideas of household responsibilities limited his participation with food to eating?

It is now a forward-thinking food philosophy for all members of a family to participate in the family food making as much as possible. But how do adults achieve that, and how do they designate responsibility for that?

**Interview** – Find two sets of couples, one that has been married for a long time, and another that is in that newlywed stage. Talk to the couple and learn about how they divide up kitchen duties, including grocery shopping, putting away, prepping food, preparing meals, discarding waste, and financial considerations they make. Learn as much as you can about how they agree or disagree over the food they buy through their marriage.

**Class Poll!** How many students in your class have shopped for their own food? How many go with their mother? How many shop with their father? How many are the responsible party to shop for their family? Discuss how you view purchasing food for yourself and other people, and the impact that your sex has on how you feel about it.

# NEW BUTTER FOR BISCUITS

This is a famous story in my family. My great-grandmother would have told this story exclusively in Spanish.

While the World War was winding down, rations were starting to lift from households. Being from a poor neighborhood and raising five children in a rural community meant that Juanita (my grandmother) and Dionicia (her older sister) would not only take lunch to school and work, but would have to augment their own lunch to their own standards to fit in with the cultural norms around them. The girls had moved away from taking tortillas in their lunch sack, less they be made fun of by other students, so instead, they took simple flour biscuits with peanut butter smeared in between often with a piece of fruit. One day, Dionicia had it with the biscuits. She wanted a sandwich, and her mother told her she should be happy with the biscuit she was getting. On their way out to the school bus, Dionicia took her biscuit, unwrapped it from the paper, and chucked it by a tree by the bus stop. Juanita kept her biscuit, ate it during lunch, and then when the two came home, Dionicia was hungry. She complained to her mother that she was hungry, to which she replied, "Oh, that's is odd, maybe you should go walk out by that tree over there and have a biscuit. I saw someone throwing them there earlier."

Image © Doris Rich, 2011. Used under license from Shutterstock, Inc.

# SINGLE SHOPPING

Since I'm by myself, I'll go somewhere with lots of unique ingredients that require me to read labels really closely. I will use the hand basket and carefully walk through the store, putting it down at my feet when I want to discover a food that I want to eat. I'll hold items up to the light and look at them, if there is a clerk available I will ask him a question, knowing he probably won't know the answer anyways. I look for the things I tried to offer my family but they refused, goat cheese on a baguette, pitted dried dates, and pieces of Parmesan with olives. I would put all of these ingredients in my single basket, buying the smallest sizes available, because it's all going to be just for me. I would walk around and decide carefully what to drink, because I know when I leave the store I'll have to picnic by myself so I can enjoy the food and green tea that my family thinks is "gross." Single shopping time! At first it's the only kind of shopping that you know, and then suddenly it becomes a selfish fantasy.

**Respond:** What kind of shopping experience do you have? Do you go with another person? Do you help pick out the food? How is your reality different than your fantasy?

# FUN OR TORTURE?

What kinds of foods do you think are for pleasure What is your idea of food torture?

Write about how you think the following experiences would make you feel, or how these experiences have made you feel if you have experienced them. Describe if these experiences are for more masculine or feminine roles.

Grocery shopping with Octomom and her fourteen children.

Tasting cheese and wine with a good friend.

Having cucumbers put on your eyes during a massage.

Roasting a pork shoulder on a barbeque.

Hunting rabbit in the French countryside.

Farming quail for a fine dining restaurant.

Having to press grapes with your feet to make wine.

Baking cupcakes for a classroom.

Making Thanksgiving dinner for the family.

Consult the rest of your class and decide if any of these experiences have implications based on the gender that is experiencing them.

## THE COOK ON TV

A chapter about gender and food would not be complete if we didn't talk about the array of chefs that are on television every week. The connection between the persona of the chef and the food he or she makes often reflects stereotypes and anti-stereotypes.

Chefs present themselves on television as lovers of their cuisine and promoters of their techniques, but what kinds of cooking are they talking about, who is their audience, and what is the goal of their food?

Watch any type of television cooking show and take notes on all of the gender-specific attributes you notice within the context of the show. How does the host perform his or her gender on camera, and how does it translate into the food?

© Ljupco Smokovski, 2012. Used under license from Shutterstock, Inc.

Name of Show:

Featured Chef:

Length of Program:

Number of recipes covered:

Types of techniques shown:

Ingredients used:

Other participants in the show, their gender and their roles:

Types of sponsors or specific advertisers featured on the show:

Types of commercials during the show

Now watch a cooking show that features someone of the opposite gender:

Name of Show:

Featured Chef:

Length of Program:

Number of recipes covered:

Types of techniques shown:

Ingredients used:

Other participants in the show, their gender and their roles:

Types of sponsors or specific advertisers featured on the show:

Types of commercials during the show

Discuss as a class how these shows display gender for mass audiences

# OH NO, SHE/HE DIDN'T!

Image © olly, 2011.  Used under license from Shutterstock, Inc.

Earlier in the chapter, we talked about my own issues with being a "matron" of the family, and the fact is that we have come pretty far in this world when I can write this as an American woman, and I'm not being committed to an institution because I don't love my children because I fantasize about only shopping for myself. In fact, sometimes I do, on my way home from work, while the kids are at school, and I get to take my time. But I don't HAVE to be in the kitchen. In some countries still, women are not afforded with rights to work outside the home, and at one point in time in America, this was something that was up for debate, just not for the women to debate. Things were the way they were, men hunt, women make bread. Men take train to city for money for wife's bon-bons and cake mix. And at the time, there were all sorts of arguments presented for why women needed to stay in the kitchen and why they were not fit for the workplace. Many of the arguments ended up being **fallacies.** A **fallacy** is an illogical argument, often not considered in academic circles. There are three areas of fallacy, each with unique types of fallacies for the information being presented in the argument. The following list contains only a few examples of what could become its own book of information.

Emotional

Scare tactic – When a statement creates a sense of fear in the audience.

Either-or choice – When a statement creates a black-and-white choice.

Slippery slope – When a statement proposes that if one thing happens, then another thing will happen too.

Sentimental appeal – A statement that yearns for the days of yesteryear and the emotions of the audience.

Bandwagon appeal – The appeal that if one person is doing it, then everyone should do it too.

Ethical Arguments

False authority – When the statement established authority that is false.

Dogmatism – When a statement insists that this way is the only way.

Ad hominem – When a statement is geared toward character instead of the direct topic

Logical Argument

Hasty generalization – When there is insufficient evidence for the argument that is being made.

Begging the question – Stating that the audience can't believe something because of something else.

Straw man – Reasoning that the person who made the statement is faulty because of the statement he or she made

Pretend that it is considered wrong for people of your gender to work outside the home, and instead they should be the caretakers for the children and the guards of the hearth. Create fallacious arguments to "prove" your point. (Note to instructor: Add other fallacies at the end of the chart for your specific lesson plan.

Fallacy (add others at the end!)                     Example:

| Fallacy | Example |
|---|---|
| Scare Tactics | |
| Either / Or | |
| Slippery Slope | |
| Sentimental Appeal | |
| Bandwagon Appeal | |
| False Authority | |
| Dogmatism | |
| Ad Hominem | |
| Hasty generalization | |
| Begging the Question | |
| Straw Man | |
| | |
| | |
| | |
| | |

# WHO IS SCULPTING WHAT?

The pressures to conform to body stereotypes are not limited to gender. What each gender desires is the reflection of the culture of body image that it is accustomed to. It is apparent that often foods are associated with body type.

For this exercise, grab a popular magazine about food (one that you can deface without getting into trouble). Grab some scissors and some tape or glue and cut out images that you might find in popular magazines that use food and people as a combination in advertisements or pictorials. How does the image reflect a social norm or contradiction? How is food being used as a symbol? What are the relationships present? Place them into your book and analyze the message about body type the image is giving the reader.

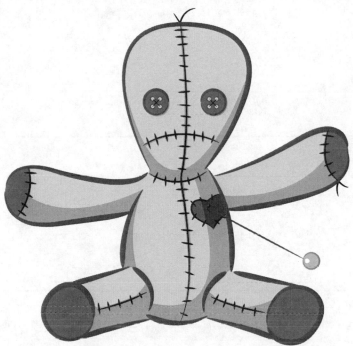

Image © dobric, 2011. Used under license from Shutterstock, Inc.

Glue Here:

Glue Here:

Glue Here:

Glue Here:

Glue Here:

## MASCULINE AND FEMININE FOODS

Are some foods more for men than for women? How can you tell?

Using the chart below, make a list of foods that you identify as being "feminine" and another you believe to be "masculine" and yet another that is labeled "androgynous." Consider the following list, and then add your own ideas!

| Feminine | Masculine | Androgynous |
|---|---|---|
| | | |

Scrambled Eggs, Bananas, Apples, New York Steak, Coffee, Hot Chocolate, Cupcakes, Pork Ribs, Tacos, Hot Dogs, Crème Brulée, Apple Pie

Discuss with your classmates: Are there particular foods that seem more gendered than others? Do people find particular ethnic foods to be for one gender or the other?

## COOKED BY HER BOOKS

The introduction of a cookbook is often the place the author not only gives the perspective of the cookbook, but also what motivated them to put together that particular collection of recipes. If the goal is to convince others of the legitimacy of their recipes how might that translate to the historically oppressed? Consider this excerpt from the cookbook, *The Perennial Political Palate,* what is the goal of this text?

# INTRODUCTION

## ON PERSISTENCE AND FEMINISM

A perennial is a plant which dies down to the ground each winter and then returns to life in the spring, the roots being the maintaining force of life.[1] In contrast an annual is one which flowers, sets seed in a season and dies. The word perennial, from per-annum means through the years. Bloodroot the plant is a perennial. Bloodroot, the feminist restaurant and bookstore has survived sixteen winters, sustaining her owners' feminist vision as well as keeping minds and bodies fed.

There is much talk these days in academic circles of the first and second waves of feminism, as well as the possibility that we are now entering a third. In these circles, the implications are that the struggle for women's suffrage was a distinct beginning, starting in the latter part of the nineteenth century and completed in the early part of the twentieth; and that a second consciousness arose in the late sixties until the mid-eighties. Of course, a careful perusal of women's writings that managed to make it into print and survive shows that feminism has existed through the years.[2] Feminism is a perennial. Regardless of which wave patriarchal time assumes us to be in, feminist roots have always existed, as evidenced by women in resistance. There have always been women who wouldn't accept what men wanted of them, always women who fought rapists, and always women who didn't want to be pregnant. There have always been women who imagined and created life without violence, war, and murder, and always women who have been healers. It's not that *all* women have been so, but there have always been *some*. There are times that seem like winter to feminists, and there are always women who tell the men what they want to hear,[3] but others resist and wait through the winter for a warming sun and spring rain. Some may die, the land being too poor, but others find fertile ground and persist.

While there is beauty to be found in annuals, gardeners do need perennials. Because we believe in return and survival, we decided to call this book *The Perennial Political Palate*. Our earlier books are *The Political Palate* and *The Second Seasonal Political Palate*.

## OUR HISTORY

In 1977 there were a number of women who felt the influence of feminism strongly enough to put their beliefs into effect, using the resources available to them, by starting feminist businesses. We were among them. It was impossible for those of us who started Bloodroot to proceed with our lives in the same way once our consciousness changed. We had to change our circumstances and hope to change those of other women as well.

For us this endeavor took the form of a restaurant and a bookstore, both "feminist." The bookstore was easy to stock; there were a growing number of feminist presses producing books of interest.[4] The restaurant would have to be vegetarian. Only by refusing to use the flesh of other creatures and therefore economizing on the earth's riches so that more might eat could we call our food feminist. It seemed appropriate to call our venture Bloodroot (the common name of a North American

---

[1] There are herbaceous perennials and shrubby perennials. The latter maintain twigs, stems and branches when leaves have dropped. There are also evergreen perennials.

[2] e.g. Virginia Woolf, especially in *Three Guineas* (New York: Harcourt, Brace, Jovanovich, 1938), Ruth Herschberger in *Adam's Rib* (New York: Pellegrini and Cudahy, 1948), and Simone de Beauvoir in *The Second Sex* (New York: Alfred A. Knopf, Inc., 1952), all writing between the so-called "waves."

[3] Such as Clarence Thomas' women friends at the Congressional hearings of his Supreme Court nomination. Since they hadn't been sexually harassed, they couldn't believe Anita Hill could have been.

[4] Feminist publishing companies active in the seventies included: Daughters Inc., Persephone Press, Diana Press, The Feminist Press, Naiad Press, Moon Books, Booklegger. The Women's Press (of England). The Women's Press (of Canada), Frog In The Well, Women's Press Collective, Speculum Press, Violet Press, Spinsters Ink, Pearlchild, Cassandra Publications, Elf and Dragon Press, Kids Can Press, New Seed Press, and Ata Books.

wildflower),[5] though the name upset some people then, and still continues to puzzle a few now. The word Bloodroot apparently connotes something disturbing to these people. We don't know why. Our blood is fed by vegetables, those that grow below ground as well as those that grow above. What can possibly be considered bad about blood? Perhaps it evokes an ancient fear of women's blood (menstruation). When customers ask, we show them a page in our first cookbook describing the plant and its manner of growth: the way the rhizomes branch, each piece sending up its own leaf furled vertically around a single flower. It was our intention to form a working collective like that, an interdependence, each separate and individual, independent but joined.

We considered ourselves radical feminist lesbians in 1977, and we still do. We didn't encounter Mary Daly's definition of radical feminism until 1984, when she wrote *Pure Lust*, but we then found it strikingly appropriate to what we were attempting. Her definition has four parts. First, a woman feels "an awesome sense of otherness from patriarchal norms and values." Second, she has a consciousness of the "sadosociety's sanctions against radical feminism." Third, she feels "rage at the oppression of all sisters of all races, ethnic groups, and nations—an identification with woman as woman." And finally, a radical feminist persists despite the odds, when others decide that feminism is a phase that has passed, or that it is out of 'fashion.'[6]

The question was (and still is), how does one take these words and put them into concrete action? We needed to do that. The word that best described our state of mind in 1977 was desperate. We *had* to make a change, for our souls' sake. We were determined—even though we had no business skills to speak of. It took a leap of faith (and some money) to do something we felt we had to do. It was our sense of otherness that required us to set aside caution and do something radical with our lives.

Those who took primary responsibility for Bloodroot have changed through the years, though there are three who have persisted. Many have come to work part-time, and left, and some work part-time and have stayed. Sometimes the leavings have been painful. When we work hard with each other, laugh at the same jokes, argue, and learn from each other's lives, of course we love those with whom we have grown in struggle. Sometimes the separations are sad, but not painful. That's how it is in the garden, in the restaurant, and in our lives. We can't imagine otherwise.

## PLACE

We cherish a small piece of land on an inlet of Long Island Sound in Bridgeport, Connecticut. Bridgeport is an extreme example of an industrial city suffering seriously from the callous and selfish economic practices of the eighties, as well as earlier times. The city is largely African-American, Latina, and Asian. Its riches are in its cultural diversity, its strong, outspoken people. We are proud to be a part of it. Yet a few years ago, an entrepreneur across the harbor decided that the city should take our land by eminent domain so that he could expand his amusement-park ideas of what is good for Bridgeport. Luckily, neighbors joined us to defeat the proposal, so our waterfront still remains beach plums and shore roses, which we planted over the broken cement fill dumped there by an earlier owner. (Some say we have persisted like the roses, complete with thorns, which thrive over the broken cement.)

More recently, representatives of the sadosociety attempted to build a regional medical waste plant right next to a city housing project, to further pollute our air. There are also continued attempts to make Bridgeport the garbage incineration center of the Northeast. Many people in Bridgeport, ourselves among them, struggle to keep those perversions under control. Bridgeport's financial problems and past inept leadership have been a problem to all in the area. These are issues we can't ignore; we are all affected.

---

[5] The drawing of the bloodroot flower that we use as our logo is the work of botanic artist Laura Louise ("Timmy") Foster. She and her husband Lincoln Foster tended what was arguably the most beautiful wildflower garden in the world on Canaan Mountain in Northwest Connecticut. Both now deceased, their love of the earth and its plants, as well as their intelligence and generosity remain a gift to us.

[6] Daly, Mary. *Pure Lust: Elemental Feminist Philosophy*, Boston: Beacon Press. 1984; pp. 396–397.

In 1977 we started Bloodroot in Bridgeport in what had once been a machine shop. It took about three years after we opened before people came to us in enough numbers to make a livelihood possible. Many of those who came and continue to come most frequently, make it clear that the sense of otherness that inspired us to start a place like Bloodroot is something they feel too. We are constantly heartened by them. We enjoy an unusually high repeat business. We seem to be an oasis for many.[7] Because we don't wait tables, a customer places her or his order at the desk, gives their name which is written at the top of the slip, then takes the slip to the counter separating the kitchen from the dining room. When the meal is ready, the name is called, and the meal picked up. Customers are asked to clear their own tables. This procedure encourages informality and a feeling of parity which obviously pleases those who return often, and keeps away those who don't care for this kind of atmosphere. Of course, provision is made for those who do need assistance.

## PURPOSE

People often remark, when they return after several years absence, that the consistency of quality is surprising. We work hard to achieve this. Persistence is important to us, not only in making our food as delicious as possible, but also in remembering our purpose. We must look at each issue in terms of a feminist overview—how women are affected by whatever happens within Bloodroot, as well as without.

Although we are concerned with both global and local issues of our planet, we are here for women; that is our purpose. It is why the word feminist appears in our logo and over our door. It is why the thirty-foot long wall that faces the view of the Sound is covered with old photographs of women. We have a bulletin board in the foyer with items of political interest to women. We play women's music whenever we are open. A sign above the kitchen opening indicates our disparagement of calorie counting, and in another sign we attempt to discuss control of unruly children without mother-blaming. We are proud that the variety of our foods, the pictures on the wall, as well as our books and the music we play reflects the diversity of women's ethnic and racial backgrounds.

We are also here for the animals. At the beginning none of us were vegetarian, but we were convinced of the importance of vegetarianism by animal rights friends.[8] For the first three years we served fish on summer weekends, but then stopped. Rather quickly our hearts followed what the mind already agreed was rational—that eating meat is wrong for its cruelty to creatures who can feel and experience pain, and wrong because it contributes to worldwide starvation, mostly of women and children. More recently we have become increasingly aware that rainforest destruction kills our Mother Earth as well. Serious worldwide environmental decline is the result of the development of global acceptance of factory-style farming and the promotion of the false idea that meat consumption is necessary for a good life.[9] We have become passionate vegetarians as part and parcel of our feminism. As a result, it is upsetting when others don't seem to be able to learn to make the connections that have become

[7] Many of our customers are men, and some also seem to feel a sense of "otherness." This is in contrast to our early days, when it was a rare man indeed who was interested in radical feminism, though there were many who assumed that feminists would share liberal values. See *Right Wing Women* by Andrea Dworkin (New York: Putnum-Perigee, 1983), for a critical analysis of this. These days there are a few books written by men that can be called pro-feminist (such as *Men On Rape* by Timothy Beneke, *Refusing To Be A Man* by John Stoltenberg, *Men Confront Pornography* edited by Michael Kimmel, and *Final Analysis* by Jeffrey Masson), and better yet, some men are reading them and wanting to actively change themselves as well as other men. We like to believe we reinforce feminist values in men who are different and who are struggling to reject sexism.

[8] Priscilla Feral and Jim Mason initially inspired our decision to be vegetarian. Both are animal rights activists still. Jim Mason is one of the exceptional men who has tried to make the connections between oppressions. The author of *Animal Factories* (New York, NY: Crown Publishers, Paperback; 1984), he is well-read in radical feminist literature and is working on a general history/philosophy book on the origins of patriarchy and of animal domestication (as yet unnamed) to be published by Simon and Shuster. Watch for it.

[9] Worldwatch Paper 103, *Taking Stock: Animal Farming and the Environment*, July 1991. 1776 Massachusetts Ave., N.W. Washington, DC 20036. This $5.00 pamphlet is the most in-depth analysis of factory farming and the resulting global human starvation and ecological destruction that we have seen.

obvious to us. Speciesism has similarities to racism and sexism, and obvious differences (for instance, animals can't vote or lobby for themselves).

Yet racism, sexism, and speciesism all share a common denominator.[10] Our priority is not to establish which evil seems primary, but rather to set ourselves against them all in whatever ways we can. To try, anyway.[11]

As a consequence of our evolving consciousness, our menu has become less dairy-oriented. These days we are sure to offer vegan soups, salads, entrees, and desserts. We want to be sure vegans can eat well and with diversity at Bloodroot. We've altered some recipes and created many new ones. There were fifty-two vegan recipes in *The Political Palate*, fifty-five in *The Second Seasonal Political Palate*, and 138 of the recipes in this volume (85%) are dairy and egg-free. We eat and cook with less cheese, eggs, and milk. We haven't given them up altogether, but we do give pride of place to recipes that have.[12]

From the beginning, people have thought of Bloodroot as a health food restaurant. Though this might be hard to debate, it's just not where we put our emphasis. Health food fashions change. Some health food stores sell and/or serve "organic" meat, which appalls us. And there are some health food theories about which we are skeptical. When we first opened, some people would only eat whole-wheat bread. Now many ask for wheat-free bread. Some have been told that fermented foods such as soy sauce or beer or anything with yeast should be avoided. Some won't eat any foods with sweeteners in them at all, whether honey, maple syrup, or sugar. Of course we always discuss ingredients with anyone who wants to know the details of our cooking, and we are especially careful about accommodating particular allergies, but we find ourselves suspicious of prohibitions on traditional ingredients that have a long history of healthy use.

Right now fat is considered the greatest danger, not just animal fats, but oils as well. Meanwhile, there is no recognition of the long and healthy lives that Mediterranean peoples have enjoyed for centuries while liberally flavoring their food with olive oil, and there is no regard for the fact that Asian or African countries depend on palm or coconut for nourishment. A recent extensive study of 6500 Chinese people showed them low in cancer, heart disease, and diabetes until they adopted a high meat diet as in the West.[13] Yet their use of cooking oil is high. Also, in contrast to most health food "wisdom," we find calorie counting and other anti-fat activities offensive. In some of the anti-fat sentiment we find anti-fat women sentiment. This is oppressive—not only to women of size, but to all of us. Many women are forced to be anorexic or bulimic rather than be fat. Fat is virtually always a cosmetic issue, but people pretend it is a health issue.[14] It's not that we're not interested in good health; we are. But we're more sympathetic to vegan concerns than to health fashions. Of course, we try to use organic produce as much as possible. Most of all we want to use local produce in season for economic and aesthetic reasons. Just compare a strawberry or a tomato grown and ripened locally with one which has travelled across the country.

---

[10] "All of us, women and men alike, are conditioned to conform to this culture. Men are trained to be dominators, women to be subordinates. No one is exempt" writes Kay Leigh Hagan in her article "Orchids In The Arctic" in *Ms. Magazine*, Vol. 11, No. 3. The common denominator in these various oppressions is a dominator. For further reading, see *The Dreaded Comparison, Human and Animal Slavery* by Marjorie Spiegel (New York: Mirror Books, 1988).

[11] It is heartening to have books such as Carol Adams' *The Sexual Politics Of Meat, A Feminist-Vegetarian Critical Theory* (New York: Continuum Publishing, 1991), as well as organizations such as Feminists for Animal Rights (P.O. Box 10017, North Berkeley Sta., Berkeley, CA 94709), and Ecofeminist Visions Emerging (40 West 46th Street, NYC, NY 10036). The book and the organizations make the connections that we are trying to make, as has Josephine Donovan in *Signs*, Vol. 15, No. 2. "Animal Rights and Feminist Theory." To subscribe to FAR (Feminists for Animal Rights), write to Batya Bauman, P.O. Box 694, Cathedral Sta., New York, NY 10025.

[12] The argument for a vegan diet is convincingly made in *For The Vegetarian In You* by Billy Ray Boyd, (San Francisco: Taterhill Press, 1987).

[13] As reported in The New York Times, Tuesday, May 8, 1991.

[14] See *The Obsession: Reflections on the Tyranny of Slenderness* by Kim Chernin (New York: Harper and Row, 1981), and *Shadow on a Tightrope*, edited by Lisa Schoenfielder and Barb Weiser (San Francisco: Aunt Lute, 1983), for more information on fat oppression.

All of us garden, although there's no way we can produce enough for our restaurant even though our gardens are fairly large. The best use of our earth is for herbs and a few lettuces, squash, and tomatoes. It is necessary to get our hands in the earth each year, to try to figure out what She will grow with us, whether it is the garlic leaves and shiso, the blueberries which take so long to pick, or the daisies and the butterfly weed, the poppies and the nigella ("Love-in-a-mist": the source of czerniska seed for our rye bread). This past summer we were blessed with an abundance of kale for soup, an endless supply of Chinese cabbage for salads and stir-fries, generous amounts of Swiss chard, green beans, tomatillos (for Salsa Verde), and elderberries, tomatoes, cucumbers, and pears!

## ECONOMICS

It has been hard for women who want to change the unfair economic realities of patriarchy to think practically about how to make a business viable. The long hours of labor needed to make bread, to chop vegetables for soup, to devise our always changing menu, and the endless hours needed to wash dishes, dishes, dishes, don't support for long the form of thinking that says "food should be cheap." While our prices are substantially lower than other restaurants in our area, we do have to factor in enough so that we can make a decent living and pay a fair wage. We love the political conversations we have while chopping onions, but we also need time for ourselves, and the wherewithal to support it.

Within the women's community there have been many discussions about class.[15] These are often confusing as we try to understand our differences. We all differ in regard to our backgrounds: our families' access to money, their attitudes and ethical/political values, and their ethnicity or race. As each of us reflect on where we have come from (of course with strong emotion), we attempt to understand and perhaps to force ourselves into a particular class category. Here at Bloodroot we have begun to think it is not possible to fit complex individual experiences into a Marxist structure. For example, where should we slot any of the past or current ethnic peoples who immigrated here, be they Jewish, Italian, Chinese, or Thai, who started or are now opening "family" businesses? Are they capitalists, petit bourgeois, or working class?

Women who grew up poor or who see their childhoods as disadvantaged for one reason or another have spoken of their pain as well as their pride. And women who had more advantages often feel guilty. Those of mixed backgrounds, who find it difficult to fit their experience neatly into a category, may vacillate between guilt and resentment. It is necessary to remember that each of our histories is a mix of painful memories and treasured strengths. We must listen to each other to appreciate our very different points of view and behavior, the hurt as well as the pride.

It is also important to assess how we live today. Women can't be blamed for wanting to live better lives now, and it would seem feminism ought to mean that women should have equal access to the same money and power that men have. Obviously, women in the professions can make good use of their abilities to remember women whose choices are limited (see what Catherine MacKinnon makes of law, Mary Daly of academia, Phyllis Chesler of therapy, or Gena Corea of medicine),[16] but becoming a professional can also destroy or undermine a woman's loyalty to her own kind. Virginia Woolf wrote compellingly about this in *Three Guineas*.[17] Women who join the ranks of the professions must be especially cautious about being co-opted by those most responsible for the destruction of our spirits and of all that we value as feminists.

---

[15] See Vol. 4, No. 2, *Lesbian Ethics* edited by Jeanette Silveira (P.O. Box 4723, Albuquerque, NM 87196: 1991) for a recent and extensive discussion.

[16] Books by MacKinnon include *Feminism Unmodified* (Cambridge, MA: Harward University Press, 1987) and (with Andrea Dworkin) *Pornography and Civil Rights* (Durham, N.C. Southern Sisters, Inc., 411 Morris Street, 27701, 1988). Books by Daly include *Beyond God The Father* (Beacon Press, 1973), *Gyn/Ecology: The Metaethics of Radical Feminism*, 1978, *Pure Lust*, op. cit., *Websters' First New Intergalactic Wickedary of the English Language*, 1987, all Beacon Press, and *Outercourse*, 1992, Harper, San Francisco, Books by Chesler include *Women and Madness*, New York: Avon Books, 1972; *Mothers on Trial: The Battle for Children and Custody* (New York: McGraw-Hill, 1986), and *The Sacred Bond* (New York: Times Books, 1988). Books by Corea include *The Hidden Malpractice, The Mother Machine and The Invisible Epidemic: The Story of Women and AIDS*, (New York: Harper Collins, 1992).

[17] Woolf, op. cit.

It would seem that there are two possible courses of action for a feminist woman living in the patriarchy. One is to join it, to try to learn its rules and then subvert it from within, to be what Monique Wittig[18] called (speaking of writing and language) a Trojan horse. And so women become doctors, lawyers, administrators, or run for Congress, finding careers in fields previously entirely male. Hopefully when we exist in those categories in enough numbers we will make a significant difference. Unfortunately, right now most women trained in patriarchy's ways internalize patriarchal values. It is not impossible to imagine a radical feminist professional, but in practical terms, it is of infrequent occurrence.

There is another route a woman can take. She can decide to remain outside the patriarchy as much as she can, the better to critique it. But then the problem is that there is no format, no formulated "way" to proceed to make one's living and to keep our spirits healthy and whole. In contrast one can decide to become a lawyer or a doctor and learn what routes, though difficult and costly, to take to get to those goals. But to survive and not become a "professional," we have fewer or no choices. One can get a factory job or clean houses or do computer work, but find little or no satisfaction or gratification in that work.

Outside the context of these non-choices, we must realize that there is another parallel world in which women form community and do work unvalued and uncounted by the patriarchy, and unvalued though considered necessary even to women ourselves.[19] This is true globally, as is discussed by Marilyn French in *The War Against Women*. And so we are unaware of the understructure of all societies and how it is that women maintain while so many men destroy. In modern times liberal forces are undermining whatever hegemony women have had in places such as Africa or India by naming men as heads of households, and by devising cash crop systems thinking this will help alleviate poverty. What it does is give the men more power and money and leaves women, whose responsibility is always the family and community, less resources and less land to plant or from which to forage.[20]

Those invisible women we have been taught to disdain, conventional women of the old traditions, had areas of power, respect, magic—precious and sustaining where they existed. Those of us who live with "progress" have all but lost access to those resources, and modern women have been taught to hold these "old wives' tales" of myth and ritual in contempt. When we imagine where one might find guidance, we can think of ancient women—some of whom set themselves apart from the community, whether as healers or as weird old women. In Western culture we called them witches; native peoples called them shamans. Sometimes there were communities in which women managed, even if briefly, to be self-sufficient: such as the Beguines in Europe's Middle Ages or the marriage resisters' communities in pre-communist China (who possessed their own language, inexplicable to men.)[21]

For sustenance, for the sacred in today's world, modern women may be able to find resources in traditional women's work. These forms of labor use very simple technologies which require patience and

---

[18] *The Straight Mind and Other Essays* by Monique Wittig (Boston: Beacon Press, 1992) is a collection of most provocative writings.

[19] Women are invisible to ourselves. Note the prevalence of the word "guys" to address a room full of women.

[20] See Worldwatch Paper #110 *Gender Bias: Roadblock to Sustainable Development* by Jodi L. Jacobson (1776 Massachusetts Ave., N.W. Washington, DC 20036: 1992), and *The War Against Women* by Marilyn French (New York: Summit Books, 1992). Also Vandana Shiva, in *Staying Alive: Women, Ecology and Development* (London: Zed Books, 1989) argues that modern scientific knowledge and economic development intentionally destroy the earth and women's livelihood. "People are perceived as poor if they eat millets (grown by women) rather than commercially produced and distributed processed foods sold by global agri-business. They are seen as poor if they live in self-built housing made from natural material like bamboo and mud rather than in cement houses. They are seen as poor if they wear handmade garments of natural fiber rather than synthetics. Subsistence, as culturally perceived poverty, does not necessarily imply a low physical quality of life." (p. 10) She explains the failure of the "green revolution" and why famine is becoming increasingly widespread after traditional ways of staying alive are destroyed by "development" and "progress." The pamphlet and both books are must reading for feminists in that the discussion treats of women's situations in other countries and across class lines.

[21] See *A Passion For Friends* by Janice G. Raymond (Boston: Beacon Press, 1986), and The New York Times: November 1991: "A Secret Language For Women": "Called everything from "the witches' script" to the first language of women's liberation, the flowing ideographs were passed from mother to daughter in a secret literary tradition that defied China's male-dominated establishment. The script, known as "nushu" or "women's calligraphy," has all but disappeared, surviving only among a dwindling handful of elderly women in one county of a mountainous Hunan province. Nushu, made up of 2,000 individual characters, has been used by women in Hunan for at least 1,000 years."

a lifetime of study. In our industrialized world there are still a few places for a gatherer of wild herbs to go, and there are still basketmakers. Some women learn to be potters, some tend gardens and there has been a return to spinning and weaving. And women have always been knitters.

It's very difficult to explain why these activities, these kinds of work are so gratifying to those who are trying to remember how to do them. Perhaps Paula Gunn Allen's description of the word "mage" (one who does magic) in *Grandmothers of the Light* is the best help to understanding:

> The basic nature of the universe of power is magic: the name given to the practice of a mage. *Ma* . . . comes in variants: *ma, mo, mu, mi,* and *me.* All are versions of the same morpheme . . . and refer one way or another to the Great Mother or Great Goddess of the Indo-Germanic tradition. The Goddess, named variously Ma, Maa, or Maat, was in time demoted and even changed gender over the ages, but she is known even today in her identity as Tiamat, Aphrodite, Ishtar, Astarte, and Isis. She can be discerned in words such as mother, mom, mammary, mutter . . . Ma is the essential female syllable . . . and at its root designates mystery, mother, and myth, all feminine forces or powers. Ge, another interesting fragment, one from which words such as geology, geomancy, geas, geometry, geophysics, and geopolitical derive, is part of the name of Gea or Gaia . . . and refers to those of the Great Goddesses' powers that emanate from her planetary body . . . A mage is a shaman or medicine person who specializes in the control and application of the two aspects of the multitudinous Great Goddess(es). Magic refers to the ritual activities of a mage, . . . ritual actions that result in transformations.[22]

The two together, the earth and what women can make of it, are magic.

We want to lead our lives so that what we make of what we find on earth is magic. The way to find it is in the ritual of patiently doing, over and over, what is required of the work. Frequently a knitter is asked. "How long does it take to do that?" though that question never arises in regard to jogging, movie-going, or mall shopping. If we choose not to join the patriarchy, what are our other choices? There is no set of procedures to follow to become a conscious rebelling radical feminist. But a hunger exists which some try to feed by means of newage spirituality, sensing that what is missing is what is holy. Some study Native Americans and try to imitate a past not their own, recognizing the integrity of that culture, an integrity which still exists amongst traditional people in pockets around the world. The question is how to find traditional women's work, healing, magic, and spirit when one is not a traditional woman.

We might suggest that the very simple work of sustaining life can have magic in it when we absent ourselves from the noise and rush of progress and technology. It is work and often tedious work to prepare food each day, to tend a garden and struggle with weeds and tomato hornworms, to care for each other, children and ourselves . . . to make things, as in knitting, spinning, or weaving. When people ask about the time needed to produce a handmade object, it means they do not see that it is the act of making it which provides the "grounding," the stitch after stitch that are individual moments of possibility. That the finished product is useful and/or beautiful is an added satisfaction.[23] The training, work, and consciousness a potter, basketmaker or weaver possesses, skills with herbs and flowers or a frying pan are inherently satisfying and potentially of spiritual sustenance to the worker.

---

[22] *Grandmothers of the Light: A Medicine Woman's Sourcebook* by Paula Gunn Allen (Boston: Beacon Press, 1991), pp. 15–16.

[23] Max Allen, fabric historian, assembled an exhibition of cross-cultural weavings and needlework with an attendant book/catalog of the same title: *The Birth Symbol in Traditional Women's Art from Europe and the Western Pacific* (Toronto: The Museum for Textiles, 1981.) He discusses "primitive art" and women's work. He quotes (on p. 8) Douglas Fraser, "primitive art as it is understood today is not intended to serve aesthetic ends . . . either (these works) assist in ritual or they perform a social role . . . Thus the Western idea of art for art's sake would mean little to the primitive artist." He then quotes Joseph Fischer's *Threads of Tradition—Textiles of Indonesia and Sarawak:* "Labor saving devices for producing traditional cloths would be by definition meaningless . . . In traditional terms there are no short-cuts to producing a fine textile." Finally, quoting William Irwin Thompson's *The Time Falling Bodies Take to Light* (1981) about the time of Goddess worship: "Women may look to a golden age of close, intimate, and peaceful village life, but men tremble in visions of asphyxiation and extinction in the herd. As C.S. Lewis has expressed the male nightmare: 'You may add that in the hive and the anthill we see fully realized the two things that some of us most dread for our own species—the dominance of the female and the dominance of the collective.' Man cut the umbilical cord to the Great Mother with a sword, and the sword has been hanging over his head ever since."

These activities are not, in our opinion, art. Patriarchal art is not supposed to be utilitarian. An artist expects that art lives in galleries and museums. An artist cannot help but partake of a world of elitism and a defense of pornography. The hierarchical structure of art and women's gratitude for crumbs of recognition leads many women artists into a defense of violence and cruelty, and a few to attempt to imitate it. Of course there are artists who produce work that is very moving to us, just as there are doctors who can sometimes help despite their training in dissociation and in treating the body as a battleground. It is a matter of joining the ranks of "educated men," as Virginia Woolf wrote in *Three Guineas*, whose values are individual and competitive, money-oriented and worshipful of violence. Art that "sells" will be rife with those values. And "artists," women among them, will defend it all as "art."

Consider: Art and Sex as the icons of the twentieth century—not to be criticized (beyond criticism).[24]

We try to stay outside the corridors of patriarchal power as much as possible. In fact, we believe the best way to have some measure of independence within the patriarchy is by creating a small business and we would encourage other women to do likewise. It is a means of making, at least to a degree, our own reality, and of attracting and encouraging others with similar values. But whether we choose professionalism or less admired work, we believe women hunger for and miss work that has meaning and integrity. If we can imagine women living in an older time or indigenous women living in areas all over the world now where "technology" is simple, then we can imagine work that maintained a woman's life and that of the community as being at least sometimes sacred, no matter how difficult.

We are constantly told that solutions to emptiness will be found in "progress," meaning more complex technologies; and then we don't realize that what we miss is the human element and what is real in the natural world. The work that is ordinary can be magical: saved seed sprouting and growing into food; sheep's wool or flax stalk being spun into a thread and that thread forming warp into which weft can be interlaced; clay-earth shaped into a container; strips of weeds or bark bent into a shape to carry. These "hard," tedious, repeated labors aren't necessarily sacred per se, but can bring us into a consonance with our lives on earth in an appropriate way. To quote again from Paula Gunn Allen:

> This brings me to the matter of the relation of ritual magic to women's lives and especially to the women's tradition: magic, as the word itself implies (ma-ge[c], is primarily a womanly enterprise. Its closest kin are the domestic arts, and its chosen implements and procedures most closely resemble those developed by women to facilitate their tasks. It should surprise no one that the modern age, from its beginnings in the Renaissance to the present, has become more and more intensely patriarchal over the world and thus more and more thoroughly separated from womanity, from ritual magic, from tribal social systems, and from harmony with the earth. The four have ever danced together: woman, magic, tribes, and earth, and the dance goes on, even yet.[25]

## TIME AND TECHNOLOGY

Time. Our time on earth is limited. If we spend time at work which robs us of all it can and gives nothing back, how many hours each week are lost? If we relax by numbing our minds with a machine like television or with computer games, then both work and "relaxation" time are lost to us forever. We think we have all the time in the world and are entitled to all the earth's resources. It is sad that we indiscriminately waste both. Much has been written about technology and its destructiveness to the environment, much less on its effects on our souls. The truth is our lives are limited, as are the earth's riches.

Consider another cookbook within your reach—how does the Introduction reflect the goal of the author—does this change for male and female authors? Bring examples to class and discuss the motivations of cookbook authors and how their gender impacts their recipe selections.

---

[24] Some would add the media. In the December 1992 issue of *off our backs*, nikki craft wrote an article called "So Much Slime So Little Time" in which she says. "The media is the new church; the television its altar; the images its sacrament; the First Amendment its bible; and any critique its blasphemy."

[25] Gunn Allen, op. cit., p. 24.

## ASSIGNMENT 1

Write an essay in which you describe the role of the genders and their interaction with food. Are there rules or decorum that each should follow? How have your ideas been formed, and by whom? Write an essay that explains your description with support from popular culture and media.

## ASSIGNMENT 2

Choose an advertising campaign that is overtly aiming at a specific gender. Analyze how this campaign attempts to sway a particular gender to purchase its products. Study the spokesperson associated with campaign, the types of language cues used, and the props and settings used for the message.

# VOCABULARY

**Gender Role** – The societal expectation for behavior and role based on a perceived gender.

**Fallacy** – An illogical argument

# Combination Plate

## PLATE MAKEUP

I believe that one of the most important aspects of this book should be saved for last. We are all a symbolic plate of food. Throughout our lives different kinds of food are plated on us; sometimes we accept and eat, sometimes we reject. But those instances of accepting and rejecting become more difficult when we think of the attachment to the connections between ethnicity, identity, and food.

My husband's family, third-generation Anaheimers, were devoted to two restaurants in the city, an older chain barbeque place located not too far down the street from a chicken pie shop. Both of these places played vital roles in the food realities of my in-laws. They felt like these places were part of their social history, and the happiness in their faces when we all congregated as a family in the booths or devoured the takeout in the kitchen was priceless. Even if I wasn't into it, I went and smiled and chose wisely off the menu.

But time doesn't stand still, and neither does the food continuum. Anaheim is different now than it was in 1975 or 1995. With every passing decade, there is a new crop of places to eat that reflects the surrounding communities. Sometimes places stick around for decades; sometimes they die off before their first anniversary. Recently, the barbeque spot was denied a lease renewal and would be replaced. It closed on New Year's Eve; we ate there twice before their doors were locked. The replacement to the beloved barbeque ribs and chicken fried steak was a Filipino drive-thru; it would be the first to open in Orange County. During the closing, there was slight outcry from the faithful, feeling like their original notion of regional Anaheim food was diminishing and changing.

The reality is that this is happening all over the world. People often talk about language as something that is always changing, and how language is affected by all of the different influences—pop culture, necessity, usage, and the speed of the Internet. The same thing happens with food and ethnicity. No matter who you are, you might identify certain foods as being owned by your particular culture. These might be learned through childhood or part of a purposeful teaching by your parents. While this is all well and good, there is still the question about the realities of the movement of people and how they acclimate in their homelands by creating new foodscapes within their communities.

It was once an argument made by my grandmother, that in order to get along in Anaheim, or Orange County for that matter, she would be digging up and composting a certain amount of her Mexican roots. In order to assimilate into the mainstream culture, she remained concerned with how she could access foods from what she felt was an essential part of herself, her enchiladas, tamales, and *albondigas*, while Americanizing them for her culturally mixed family. On the other side of town, my in-laws were enjoying the emergence of major grocery stores and commenting on the number of *taquerias* were opening up in areas of Anaheim that were normally hosting basic Italian eateries. But today's Anaheim is a bastion of multiplicity, complete with an Arabic row that boasts falafel and pita, the acceptance of Mexican food is no longer a topic of discussion, but rather a given. One ethnicity's progress becomes another's encroachment.

**Research:** How many different types of ethnic eating experiences occur in your town? Do you have festivals that highlight particular religious ways of eating, specific cultural opportunities for trying another culture's food? Research the opportunities in your area, and note the demographics of the same area. Are there more for outside cultures or cultural norms?

As mentioned previously, the Filipino fast food place slated to take over the older place brought forth some angey comments on blogs. What is Filipino food anyway? One blogger examines how often the nature of what is perceived as ethnic food might not be as ethnic when it is marketed to the masses, despite the grumblings when the original storefront was closed down, the current store is thriving within the community.

(http://blogs.ocweekly.com/stickaforkinit/2010/12/jollibee_a_reflection_of_fast-.php)

# I WOULD NEVER EAT THAT!

But if you grew up on it, your grandma made it for you, your Dad relished it and shared it, or you become part of the preparation, you might find yourself in the position of being judged by what you eat. Often the way that groups of people are marginalized as "the other" in their community is by the food they eat. Consider this prideful poem by Paul Laurence Dunbar (1872–1906), he uses his colorful dialect to write this ode to one of his favorite foods.

# POSSUM

Paul Laurence Dunbar

Ef dey's anyt'ing dat riles me
An' jes' gits me out o' hitch,
Twell I want to tek my coat off,
So's to r'ar an' t'ar an' pitch,
Hit's to see some ign'ant white man
'Mittin' dat owdacious sin—
W'en he want to cook a possum
Tekin' off de possum's skin.

W'y dey ain't no use in talkin',
Hit jes' hu'ts me to de hea't
Fu' to see dem foolish people
Th'owin' 'way de fines' pa't.
W'y, dat skin is jes' ez tendah
An' ez juicy ez kin be;
I knows all erbout de critter—
Hide an' haih—don't talk to me!

Possum skin is jes lak shoat skin;
Jes' you swinge an' scrope it down,
Tek a good sha'p knife an' sco' it,
Den you bake it good an' brown.
Huh-uh! honey, you 's so happy
Dat yo' thoughts is 'mos' a sin
When you 's settin' dah a-chawin'
On dat possum's cracklin' skin.

White folks t'ink dey know 'bout eatin',
An' I reckon dat dey do
Sometimes git a little idee
Of a middlin' dish er two;

But dey ain't a t'ing dey knows of
Dat I reckon cain't be beat
W'en we set down at de table
To a unskun possum's meat!

**Discussion:**
How does the presentation of his topic alter the way you view the food? Is there a connection for the reader to want to avoid this food? Is there a comparison that you can make with a food that you would not eat because it reminds you of this poem? Share with the class how this work affects your idea of what you might decide to never eat.

# MY FOOD IS BETTER THAN YOUR FOOD

This comment is often heard around a dinner table when someone feels like his or her food has an edge over someone else's based not on taste, but because his or her notion is that his or her ethnic food is better. But, what is not often recognized is that the placement of cultural food standards in hierarchies has been happening for centuries. People are often classified by the foods they eat. Can you think of any examples?

Image © Norman Chan, 2011. Used under license from Shutterstock, Inc.

Image © krechet, 2011. Used under license from Shutterstock, Inc.

Image © andrej_sv, 2011. Used under license from Shutterstock, Inc.

Image © BW Folsom, 2011. Used under license from Shutterstock, Inc.

**Respond:** What would be a food that you would identify as representing your ethnicity?
**Draw it!**

When people share space, their shared cultures and customs often reflect through the plate. When Frederick Douglas writes about the availability of food in his first-person experience of growing up enslaved, he draws paradigms within the culture of slavery for who was treated with preference through the plate. The ability for workers within the house to get better food than the outside workers also creates a dividing line within the same culture.

# MY BONDAGE AND MY FREEDOM

Fredrick Douglass

As a general rule, slaves do not come to the quarters for either breakfast or dinner, but take their "ash cake" with them, and eat it in the field. This was so on the home plantation; probably, because the distance from the quarter to the field, was sometimes two, and even three miles.

The dinner of the slaves consisted of a huge piece of ash cake, and a small piece of pork, or two salt herrings. Not having ovens, nor any suitable cooking utensils, the slaves mixed their meal with a little water, to such thickness that a spoon would stand erect in it; and, after the wood had burned away to coals and ashes, they would place the dough between oak leaves and lay it carefully in the ashes, completely covering it; hence, the bread is called ash cake. The surface of this peculiar bread is covered with ashes, to the depth of a sixteenth part of an inch, and the ashes, certainly, do not make it very grateful to the teeth, nor render it very palatable. The bran, or coarse part of the meal, is baked with the fine, and bright scales run through the bread. This bread, with its ashes and bran, would disgust and choke a northern man, but it is quite liked by the slaves. They eat it with avidity, and are more concerned about the quantity than about the quality. They are far too scantily provided for, and are worked too steadily, to be much concerned for the quality of their food. The few minutes allowed them at dinner time, after partaking of their coarse repast, are variously spent. Some lie down on the "turning row," and go to sleep; others draw together, and talk; and others are at work with needle and thread, mending their tattered garments. Sometimes you may hear a wild, hoarse laugh arise from a circle, and often a song. Soon, however, the overseer comes dashing through the field. "*Tumble up! Tumble up*, and to work, work," is the cry: and, now, from twelve o'clock (mid-day) till dark, the human cattle are in motion, wielding their clumsy hoes; hurried on by no hope of reward, no sense of gratitude, no love of children, no prospect of bettering their condition; nothing, save the dread and terror of the slave-driver's lash. So goes one day, and so comes and goes another.

The close-fisted stinginess that fed the poor slave on coarse corn-meal and tainted meat: that clothed him in crashy tow-linen, and hurried him on to toil through the field, in all weathers, with wind and rain beating through his tattered garments; that scarcely gave even the young slave-mother time to nurse her hungry infant in the fence corner; wholly vanishes on approaching the sacred precincts of the great house, the home of the Lloyds. There the scriptural phrase finds an exact illustration; the highly favored inmates of this mansion are literally arrayed "in purple and fine linen," and fare sumptuously every day! The table groans under the heavy and blood-bought luxuries gathered with pains-taking care, at home and abroad. Fields, forests, rivers and seas, are made tributary here. Immense wealth, and its lavish expenditure, fill the great house with all that can please the eye, or tempt the taste. Here, appetite, not food, is the great *desideratum*. Fish, flesh and fowl, are here in profusion. Chickens, of all breeds: ducks, of all kinds, wild and tame, the common, and the huge Muscovite; Guinea fowls, turkeys, geese, and pea fowls, are in their several pens, fat and fatting for the destined vortex. The graceful swan, the mongrels, the black-necked wild goose; partridges, quails, pheasants and pigeons; choice water fowl, with all their strange varieties, are caught in this huge family net. Beef, veal, mutton and venison, of the most select kinds and quality, roll bounteously to this grand consumer. The teeming riches of the Chesapeake bay, its rock, perch, drums, crocus, trout, oysters, crabs, and terrapin, are drawn hither to adorn the glittering table of the great house. The dairy, too, probably the finest on the Eastern Shore of Maryland—supplied by cattle of the best English stock, imported for the purpose, pours its rich donations of fragrant cheese, golden butter, and delicious cream, to heighten the attraction of the gorgeous, unending round of feasting. Nor are the fruits of the earth forgotten or neglected. The fertile garden, many acres in size, constituting a separate establishment, distinct from the common farm—with its scientific gardener, imported from Scotland, (a Mr. McDermott.) with four men under his direction, was not behind, either in the abundance or in the delicacy of its contributions to the same full board. The tender asparagus, the succulent celery, and the delicate cauliflower; egg plants, beets, lettuce, parsnips, peas, and French beans, early and late; radishes, cantelopes, melons of all kinds; the fruits and flowers of all climes and of all descriptions, from the hardy apple of the north, to the lemon and orange of the south, culminated at this point. Baltimore gathered figs, raisins, almonds and juicy grapes from Spain. Wines and brandies from France; teas of various flavor, from China; and rich, aromatic coffee from Java, all conspired to swell the tide of high life, where pride and indolence rolled and lounged in magnificence and satiety.

Behind the tall-backed and elaborately wrought chairs, stand the servants, men and maidens—fifteen in number—discriminately selected, not only with a view to their industry and faithfulness, but with special regard to their personal appearance, their graceful agility and captivating address. Some of these are armed with fans, and are fanning reviving breezes toward the over-heated brows of the alabaster ladies; others watch with eager eye, and with fawn-like step anticipate and supply, wants before they are sufficiently formed to be announced by word or sign.

These servants constituted a sort of black aristocracy on Col. Lloyd's plantation. They resembled the field hands in nothing, except in color, and in this they held the advantage of a velvet-like glossiness, rich and beautiful. The hair, too, showed the same advantage. The delicate colored maid rustled in the scarcely worn silk of her young mistress, while the servant men were equally well attired from the overflowing wardrobe of their young masters; so that, in dress, as well as in form and feature, in manner and speech, in tastes and habits, the distance between these favored few, and the sorrow and hunger-smitten multitudes of the quarter in the field, was immense; and this is seldom passed over.

Let us now glance at the stables and carriage house, and we shall find the same evidences of pride and luxurious extravagance. Here are three splendid coaches, soft within and lustrous without. Here, too, are gigs, phætons, barouches, sulkeys and sleighs. Here are saddles and harnesses—beautifully wrought and silver mounted—kept with every care. In the stable you will find, kept only for pleasure, full thirty-five horses, or the most approved blood for speed and beauty. There are two men here constantly employed in taking care of these horses. One of these men must be always in the stable, to answer every call from the great house. Over the way from the stable, is a house built expressly for the hounds—a pack of twenty-five or thirty—whose fare would have made glad the heart of a dozen slaves. Horses and hounds are not the only consumers of the slave's toil. There was practiced, at the Lloyd's, a hospitality which would have astonished and charmed any health-seeking northern divine or merchant, who might have chanced to share it. Viewed from his own table, and *not* from the field, the colonel was a model of generous hospitality. His house was, literally, a hotel, for weeks during the summer months. At these times, especially, the air was freighted with the rich fumes of baking, boiling, roasting and broiling. The odors I shared with the winds; but the meats were under a more stringent monopoly—except that, occasionally, I got a cake from Mas' Daniel. In Mas' Daniel I had a friend at court, from whom I learned many things which my eager curiosity was excited to know. I always knew when company was expected, and who they were, although I was an outsider, being the property, not of Col. Lloyd, but of a servant of the wealthy colonel. On these occasions, all that pride, taste and money could do, to dazzle and charm, was done.

Who could say that the servants of Col. Lloyd were not well clad and cared for, after witnessing one of his magnificent entertainments? Who could say that they did not seem to glory in being the slaves of such a master? Who, but a fanatic, could get up any sympathy for persons whose every movement was agile, easy and graceful, and who evinced a consciousness of high superiority? And who would ever venture to suspect that Col. Lloyd was subject to the troubles of ordinary mortals? Master and slave seem alike in their glory here? Can it all be seeming? Alas! it may only be a sham at last! This immense wealth; this gilded splendor; this profusion of luxury; this exemption from toil; this life of ease; this sea of plenty; aye, what of it all? Are the pearly gates of happiness and sweet content flung open to such suitors? *far from it!* The poor slave, on his hard, pine plank, but scantily covered with his thin blanket, sleeps more soundly than the feverish voluptuary who reclines upon his feather bed and downy pillow. Food, to the indolent lounger, is poison, not sustenance. Lurking beneath all their dishes, are invisible spirits of evil, ready to feed the self-deluded gormandizers with aches, pains, fierce temper, uncontrolled passions, dyspepsia, rheumatism, lumbago and gout; and of these the Lloyds got their full share.

**Discussion Questions:**

- What is the "white" relationship to food in this excerpt?
- What is the signifier for how their foods are different?
- What kind of access do all of these different people have to resources?
- What are the punishments for stepping outside of their assigned food culture?
- What kinds of traditions might a slave take away with him or her from being exposed to these rules?

# WE'RE ALL THE SAME ON THE INSIDE, UNLESS YOU ARE A PERSON OF "COLOR" OR "LESS MONEY"

According to John Robbins, a noted activist for vegetarianism and veganism, and also the heir to the Baskin-Robbins ice cream company, his stance is clear on his opposition to the "junk food" diet prevalent in American society. In his online article, *Racism, Food and Health*, Robbins echoes a similar sentiment that has been resounded across America:

> The diets of people of color are typically higher in sugar, salt, fat, and refined carbohydrates. Lacking access to healthier foods, and also lacking knowledge about what diets are in fact healthier, the poor are easy prey, not only to the tobacco and alcohol sellers whose billboards pervade their neighborhoods, but to the junk food industry and the fast food chains who see these communities as markets they can readily exploit. (www.foodrevolution.org/racismfood-health.htm)

There have been several studies and exposés in the media about this; however, what would the actual cause of this be? Robbins states that communities are being exploited, but can you find evidence of this?

**Research:** Choose a city that has a diverse population. Analyze the prevalence of chain food stops and shopping options in that community. Contrast that with a community that has an exclusive, mainly white demographic. How do these communities display food identity to consumers?

City:

Surrounding Cities:

Top five demographic populations:

1.

2.

3.

4.

5.

Top five fast food chains:

1.

2.

3.

4.

5.

Top five full service restaurants:

1.

2.

3.

4.

5.

Top five grocery stores:

1.

2.

3.

4.

5.

Top five convenience stores:

1.

2.

3.

4.

5.

# SOUL FOOD AND STEREOTYPES

At the beginning of this book, we established through Brillat-Savarin's quote that what you eat tells the world what you think, what you believe, and what you participate in. As much as the fact that most people participate in a type of food system is apparent; no one is eating without this question being underneath his or her plate, but are those silly tropes about certain ethnicities having or not having edible food also be equated with the people who would identify that food themselves?

Let's see if you know any food stereotypes based on the following populations.

What would these people eat?

> African American –
>
> Sudanese –
>
> Japanese -
>
> Laotian –
>
> El Salvadorian –
>
> Mexican –
>
> Hawaiian –
>
> Australian -
>
> Lebanese –
>
> Arabic –
>
> Lithuanian –
>
> Uruguayan –
>
> Chilean –
>
> Cajun –
>
> Italian -
>
> Irish –
>
> British –
>
> White People –

Share your answers around your class to see which category had the most identical food identification. Analyze this information in your class. Why do you all think these people eat that particular food? Is there cultural evidence around you? Do you have first-hand accounts?

So, we all have some ideas about what certain people eat more than others. How do these more common ethnic cuisines become part of the fabric of larger culture?

One idea that can be infuriating to someone who feels a strong connection to his or her personal ethnic cuisine is the idea of that food being sold en masse. When other cultures are introduced to "foreign" food, their acceptance, adaptation, and acquisition can affect the original food relationship. For example, let's say you happen to identify yourself as a Mexican, and you truly eat beans with every meal from a large pot on your *mama's* stove. Does this mean that you identify yourself with the food object of beans? And likewise, since you have the closeness to the pinto bean, do you turn your nose when you eat refried out a can? Sometimes the identity of the food has a double edge, and the variables don't end with the bean. When the poet Amiri Baraka, formerly known as LeRoi Jones, is an African American writer and critic, going to college during the turbulent racial tension filled times of the mid-1900s, Baraka exhibits this frustration when he references foods he associates with his ethnicity.

# SOUL FOOD

LeRoi Jones

Recently, a young Negro novelist writing in *Esquire* about the beauties of America mentioned that one of the things wrong with Negroes was that, unlike the Chinese, boots have neither a language of their own nor a characteristic cuisine. And this to me is the deepest stroke, the unkindest cut, of oppression, especially as it has distorted Black Americans. America, where the suppliant, far from rebelling or even disagreeing with the forces that have caused him to suffer, readily backs them up and finally tries to become an honorary oppressor himself.

No language? No characteristic food? Oh, man, come on.

Maws are things ofays seldom get to peck, nor are you likely ever to hear about Charlie eating a chitterling. Sweet potato pies, a good friend of mine asked recently. "Do they taste anything like pumpkin?" Negative. They taste more like memory, if you're not uptown.

All those different kinds of greens (now quick frozen for anyone) once were all Sam got to eat. (Plus the potlikker, into which one slipped some thrown away meat.) Collards and turnips and kale and mustards were not fit for anybody but the woogies. So they found a way to make them taste like something somebody would want to freeze and sell to a Negro going to Harvard as exotic European spinach.

The watermelon, friend, was imported from Africa (by whom?) where it had been growing many centuries before it was necessary for some people to deny that they had ever tasted one.

Did you ever hear of a black-eyed pea? (Whitey used it for forage, but some folks couldn't.) And all those weird parts of the hog? (After the pig was stripped of its choicest parts, the feet, snout, tail, intestines, stomach, etc., were all left for the "members," who treated them mercilessly.) Is it mere myth that shades are death on chickens? (Deep fat frying, the Dutch found out in 17th century New Amsterdam was an African speciality; and if you can get hold of a fried chicken leg, or a fried porgie, you can find out what happened to that tradition.)

I had to go to Rutgers before I found people who thought grits were meant to be eaten with milk and sugar, instead of gravy and pork sausage ... and that's one of the reasons I left.

Away from home, you must make the trip uptown to get really straight as far as a good grease is concerned. People kill chickens all over the world, but chasing them through the dark on somebody else's property would probably insure, once they went in the big bag, that you'd find some really beautiful way to eat them. I mean, after all the risk involved. The fruit of that tradition unfolds everywhere above 100th Street. There are probably more restaurants in Harlem whose staple is fried chicken, or chicken in the basket, than any other place in the world. Ditto, barbecued ribs—also straight out of the South with the West Indians, i.e., Africans from farther south in the West, having developed the best sauce for roasting whole oxen and hogs, spicy and extremely hot.

Hoppin' John (black-eyed peas and rice), hushpuppies (crusty cornmeal bread cooked in fish grease and best with fried fish, especially fried salt fish, which ought to soak overnight unless you're over fifty and can take all that salt), hoecake (pan bread), buttermilk biscuits and pancakes, fatback, *i.e.,* streak'alean-streak'afat, dumplings, neck bones, knuckles (both good for seasoning limas or string beans), okra (another African importation, other name gumbo), pork chops—some more staples of the Harlem cuisine. Most of the food came North when the people did.

There are hundreds of tiny restaurants, food shops, rib joints, shrimp shacks, chicken shacks, "rotisseries" throughout Harlem that serve "soul food"—say, a breakfast of grits, eggs and sausage, pancakes and Alaga syrup—and even tiny booths where it's at least possible to get a good piece of barbecue, hot enough to make you whistle, or a chicken wing on a piece of greasy bread. You can *always* find a fish sandwich: a fish sandwich is something you walk with, or "Two of those small sweet potato pies to go." The Muslim temple serves bean pies which are really separate. It is never necessary to go to some big expensive place to get a good filling grease. You *can* go to the Red Rooster, or Wells, or Joch's, and get a good meal, but Jennylin's, a little place on 135th near Lenox, is more filling, or some place like the A&A food shop in a basement up in the 140's, and you can really get away. I guess a square is somebody who's in Harlem and eats at Nedicks.

From *Home: Social Essays* by Leroi Jones. Copyright © 1966 by William Morrow. Reprinted by permission.

Image © Brian Weed, 2011. Used under license from Shutterstock, Inc.

Who doesn't like chicken?

So, it wasn't as if it was illegal for African Americans in the mid-1950s to eat chicken. It is more a question of who is able to get access to chicken. And as Baraka points out, if you are stealing it, you might take some time to really enjoy it and treat it like a food that you might not ever have again, because should you be caught plucking the feathers out, then you'd be the one getting your feathers plucked out by local authorities. What was at one point in time a real risk for African Americans who were enslaved, the act of eating a whole chicken, instead of crumbs, bones, and parts, has changed as of Baraka's writing, where he notes the prevalence in his New York City community of chicken baskets all around.

## FOOD UNDER ATTACK

Just because a food is part of your cultural identity does not mean that your community will accept you or your tradition. As recently as this writing, some countries, such as the Netherlands, are banning the killing of animals in the Halal or Kosher method because of animal welfare concerns. This has caused an undercurrent of uncertainty for people who depend on this type of food.

Image © Jan-Dirk Hansen, 2011. Used under license from Shutterstock, Inc.

More specifically, consider the plight of the Makah tribe of the Pacific Northwest, who enjoy hunting and eating grey whales. Men train and earn their spot in a canoe, which rows out to sea to harpoon a single grey whale. The community uses the animal in prayer and shares the flesh with the community. With the recent immersion of television shows that feature boat-to-boat combat with whalers, how do you look upon the Makahs?

FAQ about the Makah tribe!
www.makah.com/pdfs/makahwhalingqa.pdf

Image © Paul Marcus, 2011. Used under license from Shutterstock, Inc.

Image © Paul Marcus, 2011. Used under license from Shutterstock, Inc.

## ASSIGNMENT 1

Decide what food you regularly eat would best symbolize who you are. Define yourself by a food, dish, or eating custom. Then imagine the outside community is against your food choice. Write an essay where you describe this food, what it means to you, and what you would be willing to give up to keep it as part of your diet.

## ASSIGNMENT 2

Research a food that you believe should be banned. Identify the current eaters of that food and how they would be affected by your ban Would you be able to suggest a substitute? What about the passion of the people who eat it? Are there particular industries that benefit from the consumption?

# VOCABULARY

**Makah** – A Native American tribe from the Pacific Northwest

**Anaheimer** – A person from Anaheim

**Possum** – A shortened version of opossum, which is a large North American rodent

_____

_____

_____

_____

_____